The Seton Miracles

Weeping Statues and Other Wonders

A journal of supernatural events concerning
Father James Bruse, Associate Pastor,
Saint Elizabeth Ann Seton Catholic Church
Lake Ridge, Virginia

by James L. Carney

Marian Foundation
Woodbridge, Virginia

According to the decree of the Congregation for the Teaching of the Faith, March 7, 1975, entitled "Decree Concerning the Supervision of the Bishops over Printed Matter," an express ecclesiastical imprimatur is required only for editions of the Bible and literature concerning Catholic liturgy and religious instruction.

Since the abolition of Canons 1399 and 2318 of the old Code of Canon Law by Pope Paul VI in AAS 58, 1186(1966), publications about new apparitions, private revelations, prophecies, miracles, etc., have been allowed to be distributed and read by the faithful without the express permission of the Church, provided that they contain nothing which contravenes faith or morals.

The author does not intend to anticipate the judgment of the Church regarding the holiness of any individual involved or the apparent miracles and supernatural phenomena which are reported here. In accordance with the Decree of Pope Urban VIII (1623-44), purely human credibility applies to such passages in this book. However, we do well also to remember the advice of His Holiness:

> *In cases which concern private revelations, it is better to believe than not to believe, for, if you believe, and it is proven true, you will be happy that you have believed, because our Holy Mother asked it. If you believe, and it should be proven false, you will receive all blessings as if it had been true, because you believed it to be true.*

Fourth edition, published by the Marian Foundation. Previous editions of this work were published in 1993, 1994 and 1998. Copies of this book may be ordered from the Marian Foundation, P.O. Box 2589, Woodbridge, VA 22193-2589 for $19.95 each plus $5.00 s/h. Add $1.00 for each additional book in the same order. Virginia residents include sales tax of $1.00 per book.

Library of Congress Catalog Card Number: 98-67910 ISBN: 978-0-9666234-1-3

All rights, title and interest of the author in this work have been assigned to the Marian Foundation, a nonprofit corporation organized under the laws of the State of Virginia. This assignment is made to eliminate any financial incentive of the author in the reporting of the events described in this book so that their credibility may be evaluated solely on the basis of the number and character of the witnesses and the circumstances and accompanying photographs included. The Marian Foundation is dedicated to fostering devotion to the Blessed Virgin Mary in the parish of Saint Elizabeth Ann Seton Catholic Church and wherever else the glory of God may find receptive hearts.

Cover Photo: *The cover photo of Our Lady of Medjugorje statue weeping at the SEAS's Knights of Columbus meeting on March 17, 1992 is courtesy of the talents and generosity of William T. Saunders.*

Photo: *Statue of Our Lady of Smiles in St. Elizabeth Ann Seton Church, Lake Ridge, Virginia, during one of its last reported weepings in July 1992.*

Father James C. Bruse was born on October 28, 1954, in Washington, D.C., and grew up in Marlow Heights, Maryland. He received a Bachelor of Arts degree with a major in pychology/sociology from Mary Washington College in 1976. He studied to become a priest at Mount Saint Mary's Seminary in Emmitsburg, MD, receiving a Master of Arts degree in theology in 1983. He was ordained the following year.

Father Bruse is a diocesan priest with the Diocese of Arlington. He was assigned as Associate Pastor to Saint Elizabeth Ann Seton (SEAS) Catholic Church on June 13, 1990.

DEDICATION

This work is dedicated to the Holy Mother of God, who has presented herself to us as Our Lady of Sorrows and Our Lady of Tears, and to all mothers everywhere who weep for their children.

ACKNOWLEDGMENTS

I gratefully acknowledge my numerous sources of assistance on this report.

All thanks and praise must go first, of course, to the Eternal God who loves us so much that He is willing to set aside the laws of chemistry and physics to get our attention. Beyond our dear and gracious Lord, I give thanks:

To the Blessed Virgin Mary, who has striven with limitless patience and concern in this century to awaken us to the folly of our ways, the urgent need for conversion, and to plead with us to return to a deep and abiding love of Jesus and the tenets of the Faith which He gave us.

To all who were generous enough of spirit to share their miraculous experiences with me and all the others who will read this report. Their love and sense of community provided the fuel which has revitalized the faith of others who have not been as fortunate in experiencing the evidence that God is, indeed, real and present to us here and now. Linda Christie's journal, *The Saga of Father Jim Bruse,* was exceptionally helpful in constructing this report. Besides Linda, special thanks go to Barbara Adams; Barbara and Bob Capell; Jack Christie; Ty Cullen; Sandy Fitz; Sue Farr; John Garing; Jacqueline Gordon; Marcia Grattan; Johanna and Maura Gregory; Pam Hood; Libby Lawler; Mary Mahler; Carol Ann Marino, who kept her own extraordinary journal; Carol and Emil Myskowski; Gloria O'Brien; Marie Pelletier; the late Fran Perotti and his wife, Jennifer; Joe Pevarnik; Dolores Rader; Tom and Pat Saunders; Amy and Tom Shaffer; Elizabeth Spoth; Jackie and Courtney Tucker and the late Chris Vogeding and her husband, Steve.

To Father Bruse, whose heart was always abundantly open to the thousands of persons who visited, wrote and telephoned for guidance and assistance. To see the Holy Spirit work in him has been a wonder to behold.

To my wife, Pinkey, whose love and support were unflagging and whose example, as an always friendly oasis for visiting "pilgrims" and curious parishioners, has been a perpetual reminder of our obligation to share these wonderful events with all who inquire with an open heart.

To Father Hamilton, our Pastor, who struggled to balance the requirements of a growing parish and the cautions of his bishop against the ever-present pressure to celebrate, perhaps too exuberantly, the mysterious sign language here of Our Lady's presence.

To Brian Varrieur, creator of the Marian Foundation logo, and Jason Gregory, for contributing their artistic gifts; and to all those generous and devoted persons who made financial donations to enable this book to exist.

To Kathy Braga, whose sharp eye and excellent judgment provided an important barometer for the new material in this third edition.

CONTENTS

ILLUSTRATIONS

PREFACE

WHEN STATUES WEEP

Believe that I am in the Father and the Father is in me,
or else, believe because of the works I do. Jn 14:11

"You won't believe what happened at the church today," my wife, Pinkey, said to me in a kind of off-hand manner early in the evening on January 14, 1992. She seemed unusually subdued, but since she was (and is) the Youth Minister at Saint Elizabeth Ann Seton (SEAS) Catholic Church, there were days when the challenges of her youthful constituents and other stresses in her ministry took a heavy toll. So, I was prepared to believe anything. But never in my wildest dreams would I have predicted what she was about to reveal.

"Father Jim has received the stigmata [bodily wounds replicating the five crucifixion wounds borne by Christ] and statues of the Blessed Virgin Mary are weeping at the church," she informed me quietly.

It wasn't that I did not believe her, but she was right all the same. I was not prepared for that disclosure. In fact, I was thunderstruck. Father Jim Bruse, associate pastor *vin ordinaire*, who was given a tee shirt by the SEAS youth group emblazoned "Father Flash" for the speed with which he often said Mass, singled out by God for an honor accorded Saint Francis of Assisi! It did not seem possible. Father Bruse, Fourth Degree Knight of Columbus, who seemed even younger than his 37 years. It couldn't be.

I pressed her for details. She had heard earlier that day from another staff member about the weeping and the stigmata and had immediately gone to the rectory to see Father Bruse. He explained to her that the weeping had begun with an Our Lady of Grace statue at his parents' house in Stafford on Thanksgiving Day the previous November. The stigmata came a month later on the day after Christmas, again at his parents' home, although the wounds did not fully appear on both sides of his wrists and in his side and feet until the days following. While he patiently explained these events to Pinkey, more like a bystander himself than a center of divine attention, a small plastic Madonna statue which was resting on his credenza began to cry. Not that the small religious icon was wracked with sobbing, of course, but water flowed copiously from the eyes and down the cheeks so that "crying" seemed the only appropriate term to describe what was clearly impossible for an inanimate, anhydrous object.

Since that momentous disclosure in mid-January 1992, I have seen approximately two dozen religious icons composed variously of plastic, metal, ceramic, plaster, porcelain and fiberglass weep in the same way. I have held small

Madonna statues in my hands and watched their eyes fill with tears which then rolled down their cheeks and puddled at the bases of the figures. I have seen as many as six of these little statues weeping simultaneously.

Icons were seen weeping in the rectory, in the church at SEAS, in our home when Father Bruse came to dinner (even inside a glass-enclosed cabinet), and at numerous other locations. Stained and etched glass images of the Blessed Virgin Mary have shed tears, meaning as before that a clear liquid that certainly seemed to be water flowed from the eyes of the figures. Before it was over, dozens if not hundreds of statues and images, most of them representing the Blessed Virgin Mary, wept under the scrutiny of thousands of observers. The weeping has been captured on film by professional and amateur photographers alike, even showing up on the first television broadcast about it on March 6, 1992.

Other strange occurrences took place, too, such as statues and rosaries changing colors. In one mystifying case, a small Fatima statue of Our Lady rotated its colors for nearly half an hour inside the SEAS church before 20-30 witnesses. This occurred at least twice more on successive Saturdays and had happened many times before that. Several parishioners reported seeing the "miracle of the sun," as has occurred at Medjugorje and other apparition sites, describing it in much the same way. Other parishioners saw strange, sometimes rotating, colors in the sky. They emphatically insist these were not rainbows and bore no resemblance to any rainbow they had ever seen. There have been whispered rumors of dramatic physical healings, at least two of which have been well documented.

This book presents a comprehensive report on these happenings which began less than seven years ago in the shadow of America's capital. Saint Elizabeth Ann Seton Catholic Church is located in Lake Ridge, Virginia, a residential neighborhood which forms one of the many satellite communities supporting the employment needs of metropolitan Washington, DC. It is about 25 miles from the city, due south down that commuters' nemesis: I-95. It is doubtful that there was any additional *kind* of inexplicable physical phenomena which took place here that is not reported in this book, although it is certain that there were many, many instances of similar occurrences which remain known only to those who experienced them plus a few confidantes or bystanders.

The "Journal" section of this book was mostly recorded at the time of the events noted, including some new material in this third edition which was withheld by request from earlier editions. Other reports were provided to me later. I have inserted them in the appropriate chronology. Altogether, the Journal describes an astonishing litany of supernatural activities, mostly weeping statues of Jesus and Mary, that took place intensively and widely over a period of about six months and continued on a much more localized, low-key basis for more than a year afterward. Some persons claim to still see the "miracle of the sun" and there may be other strange things happening which are simply unreported. But for purposes of this book, the relevant period is from November 1991 to May 1993.

This is not the first demonstration of weeping statues, of course, nor has it been the last. This phenomenon has been widespread throughout the entire world in this century. In a chapter following the Journal, I will discuss some of those. But it seems safe to say that the quantity, variety and duration of weeping statues and other inexplicable phenomena which were associated with Father James Bruse were not only incomparably greater than any other similar display in history, but may actually have exceeded all of the others put together. Add to that the dramatic supernatural event of the stigmata being imposed upon a Catholic priest, only the second time in history that has occurred,[1] and one can only conclude that God sent a virtual clarion call to humanity, certainly to America. We will consider hereafter what that clarion call, delivered through the Mother of God, might mean; in fact, what it certainly must mean.

This book, as I believe the weeping statues and other phenomena themselves were, is intended primarily for the skeptical, the worldly, the disbelieving, the doubtful, the uncomprehending and the searching. Of course, the message is vital for everyone and the faith enhancement is powerful even for those who are already devout. But, as Jesus said when questioned about his willingness to eat with tax collectors and other disreputables in his Jewish society, *"People who are healthy do not need a doctor; sick people do. I have come to call sinners, not the self-righteous."*[2] In a subsequent chapter, I will speak directly to the various criticisms and challenges put forth against the weeping statues and other phenomena in Lake Ridge and elsewhere. But even those blessed with a strong Christian faith will find much here to ponder and appreciate. Sadly, as usual, those who will not look, shall not see, and those who refuse to listen, will not hear. Deadened hearts are not moved by tears, even tears of blood.

Without question, the single most unfortunate aspect of this enormous favor from the Lord has been the misunderstanding which has arisen from the response of the bishop of the Diocese of Arlington, in whose jurisdiction most of it occurred. Father Bruse is a priest of the Arlington diocese. As you will discover from the Journal, Bishop John R. Keating first learned of the weeping statues and

---

[1]Padre Pio of Italy was the first; he received his stigmata in 1918. Saint Francis of Assisi was not a priest nor were any of the other 300+ stigmatics when they first received their wounds, except Padre Pio.

[2]Mk 2:17.

Father Bruse's stigmata wounds on January 2, 1992, in a phone call from our pastor, Father Daniel Hamilton. The next day, Father Hamilton brought him the small (about 8" high) St. Elizabeth Seton statue which had wept apparent blood, and was still stained with it, and the taller Fatima statue which had flooded Fr. Hamilton's dresser with its tears on New Year's eve. Bishop Keating locked the two little statues away and scheduled an early meeting with Father Bruse. He asked Father Bruse to be examined by his personal physician and a psychiatrist (see the Journal). In the meantime, the bishop counselled further observation and a continuation of the public silence. This was perplexing to many of us who knew about the events and it became an increasing source of frustration and confusion. Some of us wrote to Bishop Keating asking for his investigation. To my knowledge, no one received a reply to any of these letters. I know I did not.

The bishop obviously believed that his approach of waiting and watching was the best response to the situation, but it is difficult to reconcile with an Ordinary's duties under canon law. Father Michael Smith Foster, JCD, a canon law expert, has stated:

> *"Because the bishop is responsible for public worship in the diocese, it is his responsibility to discern what is apparently miraculous and to approve of the gathering for public worship.... Should an apparently miraculous event occur, the people may petition the bishop to investigate what is happening. If the bishop determines that there is sufficient evidence for an investigation, he should begin a process which would lead to a decision concerning the supernatural character of the event.... Above all, for purposes of regulating the liturgical life of the diocese, the bishop's responsibility is to assure that the people committed to his care are not being deceived and that something authentically miraculous has occurred, so others who wish may commemorate the sacred event in their worship. In exercising their episcopal oversight, bishops must be diligent in their search for the truth, open to the presence of the miraculous, and able to reject what is inauthentic or false.*[3]

Father Foster's article is addressed to private revelations and apparitions, but their logic applies even more to physical phenomena.

---

[3]Abridgement of "Canonical Considerations Regarding Alleged Apparitions," *Marian Studies* 46 (1995), The Marian Library, University of Dayton, Dayton, OH.

Finally, the ever-widening circle of parishioners, friends and relatives who learned of the weeping statues and Father Bruse grew to the point that the press did get wind of the matter. On March 6, 1992, the Washington CBS television affiliate, WUSA (Channel 9), broadcast the story on the 11:00 p.m. news. *The Washington Post* and considerable other national and world press followed promptly.

The day before the story broke, the Chancery stated its position on the matter in a formal declaration to Father Hamilton. The full statement is included at Appendix A, but what it said, in a nutshell, is that since there was no overt divine message being delivered, there was nothing to investigate. This was certainly a peculiar determination since *only* physical phenomena can be investigated. Reports of apparitions and locutions cannot be investigated. They can merely be assessed as to whether they are consistent with Catholic faith and morals. In fact, the validity of apparitions is almost always determined by the accompaniment of inexplicable physical signs, such as the mysterious spring and subsequent miraculous healings at Lourdes or the incredible spinning and falling sun presented to 70,000 people at Fatima. How else can God give these private revelations His seal of authenticity? Barring some internal contradiction or conflict with Catholic doctrine and traditions, only inexplicable, external evidence can provide the necessary supernatural endorsement which will permit the Church to authorize its priests and faithful to consider the event as a genuine private revelation.[4]

So the faithful in St. Elizabeth Ann Seton parish and elsewhere were left to muddle through on their own. From that moment forward, the diocesan Chancery would essentially refuse to acknowledge even that anything out of the ordinary was happening. Further, Fathers Hamilton and Bruse were told to conduct one press conference on March 12 and thereafter to say nothing else and do

---

[4]Bear in mind that the Church never folds private revelations into its formal declarations of faith. Public revelation, which includes everything necessary for our salvation and full understanding of Christianity, ended with the death of the last Apostle, John. When the Church approves a private revelation, no matter how numerous the signs or saintly the recipient, belief by the faithful always remains optional. However, there is a vast gulf between those private revelations which the Church has not declared "worthy of belief" and those which she has so pronounced. And, of course, a declaration by the Church that an alleged private revelation is "not worthy of belief" is a prohibition against any ecclesial endorsement or activity in connection with it. Hence the importance of the local Ordinary's prompt and thorough investigation of apparently supernatural physical phenomena, whether or not a "message" is overtly attached to them.

nothing further which would encourage the faithful to believe that anything miraculous was happening around Father Bruse.

Of course, the phenomena went right on, increasing in scope and variety. Thousands of people witnessed innumerable statues, icons, crucifixes, rosaries and religious medals weep or change colors, sometimes both. The secular press continued to publish numerous stories, some with photos of statues weeping, until finally its news value was exhausted. Father Bruse and Father Hamilton refused numerous requests for interviews and talk show appearances. The diocesan newspaper, the *Arlington Catholic Herald*, published a cover story on March 19, using terms like "seeped" and "produced water," and thereafter was silent on the subject.

The problem with such "stone-walling," as many politicians and others have discovered, is that just as nature abhors a vacuum, so questions seek answers, whether official or unofficial, correct or incorrect. The thousands of people who saw statues weep at various times did not need an official declaration to confirm what their eyes told them. Those who trusted in the eyewitness testimony and photographs of others were also satisfied as to the obvious Source of what was happening around Father Bruse.

But throughout the larger Church community, Bishop Keating's determination to ignore the events inevitably generated a conclusion that he had condemned them as false. Thus, we were treated to the words of author Frank Orlin Johnson, Ph.D., in his book, *Why Do Catholics Do That?, A Guide to the Teachings and Practices of the Catholic Church.*[5] Dr. Johnson, who apparently never personally interviewed Father Bruse or anyone else knowledgeable about the weeping statues in Lake Ridge, Virginia, contrasted the *"worthy of belief"* weeping in Syracuse, Sicily, in 1953 (discussed hereafter at length in the chapter on "Statue Weepings Around the World") with the *"unworthy of belief"* weepings involving Father Bruse. Using words for the Lake Ridge weepings like *"put[ting] a stop to the fuss"* and *"emotions...brought to the boil,"* Johnson contrasted the Syracuse situation (where Pope John Paul II himself dedicated the massive Shrine of Our Lady of Tears in 1994) with Father Bruse and Saint Elizabeth Ann Seton Church by saying the *"two occurrences followed the distinction between religion and superstition, between devotion and hysteria.... In Lake Ridge, nobody saw the*

---

[5]Also titled *Expressions of the Catholic Faith,* New York:Ballantine Books, 1994.

statue weep; they just saw puddles on the floor 'afterward'... Nobody was cured of anything."[6]

The point here is that people expect an investigation of the inexplicable. And one which points to God as its cause produces an expectation in the faithful that the Church will represent them in ascertaining to the best of anyone's ability whether God is manifesting Himself in some special way. He has done so countless times, either directly or through one of His saintly creations, especially the Blessed Virgin Mary, since Jesus Christ ascended to heaven. Even though these occasions add nothing to the deposit of Faith, they are continuing signs of God's love for us and His desire to help us.

Perhaps even more to the point, however, is that these occasions usually bring an important message, whether explicitly stated or not. Father Bruse and the weeping statues, etc., at Saint Elizabeth Ann Seton Catholic Church, etc., are no exception. Bishop Keating's decision to ignore the events is a mystery, a very unfortunate one. It did not leave a neutral opinion in its wake. It left a negative implication because the common response to such matters is to want to find out what is happening and why. The bishop's apparent disinterest suggested that he must know something negative about the cause of the phenomena.

As for whether a message can be divined from silent, tearful statues of the Blessed Virgin Mary, we need look no further than the words of His Holiness John Paul II, the Vicar of Christ on earth: "*The tears of the Madonna belong to the order of signs. She is a mother crying when she sees her children threatened by a spiritual or physical evil.*" As noted by Agostino Bono in his story in the *Arlington Catholic Herald*, "*[W]hen tears shed by Marian images are declared miraculous by the church, they take on an almost cosmic significance. They show concern for events past and forewarn of dangers to come. They are tears of prayer and hope.*"[7] But how can the origins be deemed miraculous if the responsible church official refuses to investigate and report?

The contents of this book provide at least an unofficial report on a dramatic, astonishing and alarming communication from heaven. All names, dates and places identified are real. None of the photographs has been retouched in any way. Father Bruse at this writing is a fully accredited pastor at his own parish in the Arlington diocese, and much beloved by his parishioners. The material presented here is offered to you as accurately as my legal training, skills of

---

[6]Pp. 157-158.

[7]Both quotes are drawn from the *Herald's* January 19, 1995 story, titled "Pope Reflects on Cosmic Meaning of Crying at Weeping Mary Site," p. 12.

expression, and powers of observation permit. Not once from the moment I learned about the statues crying and Father Bruse's stigmata wounds until this moment has there been a hint of fraud or profiteering by any person even remotely connected with the events. This book is in every sense a gift to your soul.

Your mother in heaven is crying for you.
Come back to her Son.
Come back to God.
Come home.
Dry her tears with prayers from your heart.

THE SETON MIRACLES

A JOURNAL OF SUPERNATURAL EVENTS CONCERNING FATHER JAMES BRUSE, ASSOCIATE PASTOR, SAINT ELIZABETH ANN SETON CHURCH

This journal records events and occurrences of apparently supernatural origin. Nearly all of them were either witnessed by me or reported to me by actual eyewitnesses. The manifestations which have taken place have almost always been associated directly or indirectly with Father James Bruse, Associate Pastor of the Saint Elizabeth Ann Seton Catholic Church in Lake Ridge, Virginia. The first interview took place on January 19, 1992, in Fr. Bruse's office.

FIRST OCCURRENCES

Father Bruse explained that the first event involved a small statue of Our Lady of Grace which he ordered for his mother from W. Gallery, a religious goods store in Wheaton, Maryland, shortly before Thanksgiving 1991. The statue in Figure 1, which is about 12 inches high, is a replica of this one. He had selected this statue because of its appealing appearance. He said his mother had an older statue which was now somewhat worn and he wanted to give her a new one.

When the statue arrived in the mail, he was disturbed to find it not exactly what he thought he had ordered. The expression on its face seemed more melancholy than the one in the catalog. A call to W. Gallery, however, confirmed from markings on the box that the statue was the correct one. Still, the expression on the Madonna's face seemed different to him. He explained his misgivings to his mother, and offered to exchange the small statue for another, but she insisted on retaining it.

Early in the afternoon on Thanksgiving Day, November 28, 1991, Fr. Bruse blessed his parents' house with holy water and prayer. Shortly afterward, someone noticed that the new Madonna statue had what appeared to be tears on its face. Father Bruse was skeptical. He was sure that the water must simply be drops of holy water which had been inadvertently cast on the statue. Or, perhaps the materials in the statue were reacting in an odd way to the humidity in the house. Soon, the statue was crying profusely. Father Bruse and his father both tasted the fluid flowing from the eyes. It was slightly salty, as tears would be.

Throughout the rest of that day, Fr. Bruse and his parents watched as the Our Lady of Grace statue would weep, then stop, then begin again.

The weeping continued the next day. By now the word had spread to other family members. Father Bruse's sister, Sue Farr, arrived with her two children. It was still hard to accept what was happening. His sister said, "I took my finger and wiped away the tears and they just bubbled right back out again!" She and Father Bruse were still not convinced. There must be some natural explanation, they thought.

On Saturday, November 30, Fr. Bruse's aunt and uncle arrived to see the remarkable weeping statue. They were not disappointed.

The statue continued to weep every few days, including on the Feast of Our Lady of Guadalupe (December 12). On Saturday, December 21, Mr. and Mrs. Bruse returned from a Christmas party to find that the table on which the statue rested was covered with water which had flowed onto the carpet, drenching it. They filled a jar with the water which they were able to mop up.

CHRISTMAS 1991

On Christmas day, Father Bruse celebrated Mass in his parents' home. During the Mass, the Our Lady of Grace statue began to bleed from the eyes. Later, it cried normal tears and washed the blood stains away. The statue wept profusely that day. "Every time somebody walked through the door, the statue would start crying. It would stop, somebody would come through the door, and it would start crying," according to Sue Farr.

The day after Christmas, 1991, turned out to be a very momentous one in the life of Fr. Bruse and his family. The Our Lady of Grace statue continued, as before, to weep intermittently. But now a new phenomenon appeared. Father Bruse's niece picked up a small white Fatima statue and remarked, "Boy, this really looks plain." The little statue had flesh tones and gold trim but no other colors.

Afterward, Fr. Bruse and his sister went out for awhile. Upon their return, her daughter said, "Mom, it looks like there's something green on that statue."

Sue replied, "No, it's probably just a reflection from the flowers or something." But, to be sure, she picked up the statue and carried it over to the door where the light was better. She realized the entire dress was turning green. All the family members came running over to see what was happening.

"As I held it in my hand, it turned green and orange and blue and pink. We watched the colors come!"

Since the little statue was identical, except smaller, to one which Sue had herself, she called her husband in Oxon Hill, Maryland, and asked him to go and check it. It was still white. Later that day, however, that statue also assumed a variety of colors. Calls to other relatives in Clinton, Maryland, and Vienna, Virginia, discovered that their white Fatima statues had likewise taken on pastel coloring similar to that found in other commercial versions of Our Lady of Fatima. A week or so later, a cousin in Sterling, Virginia, reported his Fatima statue had changed from white to colors and, also, that his rosary had changed its color to red. There was no natural explanation for any of these happenings.

Within the next month, additional statues would suddenly change colors or hues. The SEAS (St. Elizabeth Ann Seton) Parish Administrator, Mrs. Marie Pelletier, reported her 38-year-old Our Lady of Grace statue, which had been handed down to her from her mother, changed the white lining of its cloak to pink and the blue of its veil to a deeper bluish-purple color. This occurred after Fr. Bruse blessed it. Another Our Lady of Grace statue belonging to a friend of Fr. Bruse's mother also changed colors.

Perhaps the most dramatic thing to occur on this day of increasingly incredible experiences, however, was the receipt of Fr. Bruse's stigmata wounds and the means by which that occurred. A small Infant of Prague statue at his mother's house suddenly appeared to literally come to life. The eyes changed color and moved. The skin on the arms and hands became soft and warm to the touch. Numerous family and friends in the Bruse house that day saw this and can testify to it. Father Bruse, while attempting to straighten the robe on the little statue, received what he described as a strong electric shock. Later, his stigmata wounds began to appear.

At first, Fr. Bruse was not aware of any marks on his body. Not long after, however, three small red dots appeared on the inside of his right wrist. By the next day, the 27th of December, three small red dots appeared also on the inside of his left wrist, accompanied by a large bruise farther up the arm. The stigmata wounds on the top of his wrists did not appear until January 12, 1992.

Several statues wept in the Bruse household that day. More incredibly, at least three of them wept blood. A friend of the family who was present, engaged to be married to Fr. Bruse's aunt, had not practiced his Catholicism for many years. After this experience, he returned to active participation in the Church, sold off his business, broke his engagement and, as of Spring 1992, was looking into entering a seminary in Ireland.

Because of all the family and friends staying over that night, Fr. Bruse's sister slept in the living room. She has reported a scent of incense was present from an unidentified source during the night.

In the morning, the 27th of December, Fr. Bruse celebrated Mass in his parents' living room. Afterward, someone remembered two statues that had been stored in the attic, one of them being the Sacred Heart of Jesus and the other a Madonna statue. There was no indication that they had wept in the attic, but about an hour after they had been retrieved, the Sacred Heart statue began to bleed from its heart onto the floor. The blood stains on the light beige carpet did not remain, however. They simply vanished after a few minutes.

Early that afternoon, Fr. Bruse and his sister went to a grocery store. While there, shortly after 2:00 p.m., his feet began to hurt him severely. They discovered they were bleeding. He limped painfully back to the car and they returned home. By the time they arrived, his socks were soaked in blood. About this time, he began to experience sharp pains in his right side. The wound there also began to bleed. As he and his sister walked in, they saw that all of the statues in the living room were weeping.

By evening of that day, the family had made a definite connection between Fr. Bruse and the weeping statues. They noticed that every time he held a statue which had been blessed, it would begin to cry. Unblessed statues would start to weep after being blessed by him. He touched a picture of Our Lady of Medjugorje and tears promptly began to emerge from the eyes and run down the wall. By now, many additional family members and friends had been contacted and had come to see the amazing happenings for themselves. At least fifteen people were present at various times that evening of December 27, 1991.

Father Bruse left his parents' house on the 28th and returned to the rectory at SEAS. It was a Saturday and he was scheduled to say the 6:00 p.m. Mass. In his room, he discovered his own Fatima statue with exposed heart no longer had a plain white dress. It now had yellow highlights in it.

On December 30, 1991, Fr. Bruse visited an uncle in intensive care at a local hospital near his parents' home. While in the cafeteria there, his stigmata wounds began to bleed.

With his parents, he visited the gravesites of his deceased grandparents. When he touched the carved religious statues on the headstones, they wept.

After Fr. Bruse returned to his parents' home, the Our Lady of Grace statue wept profusely on at least three occasions. By this time, the statue had been generating so much water that Mrs. Bruse placed it in a dish to catch the tears. The water overflowed the dish and spread across the floor. Over two pints were collected.

EARLY OCCURRENCES IN SEAS PARISH

By the 28th of December 1991, when Fr. Bruse returned to St. Elizabeth Ann Seton (SEAS) to celebrate the 6:00 p.m. Mass, he was ready to confide in Father Daniel Hamilton, the pastor. By now the incidence of statues weeping was far beyond any conceivable natural explanation. Father Bruse's own Fatima statue in his room at the rectory had taken on yellow coloring in its gown while he was at his parents' house. His stigmata wounds were real, painful and bleeding. He needed guidance.

On New Year's Eve, Father Bruse told Fr. Hamilton about the weeping statues. The pastor's initial reaction was one of astonishment and disbelief. After two previous associate pastors had abruptly abandoned the priesthood altogether when they left SEAS, it now began to look as if "strike three" might be headed SEAS' way. He counseled prudence and patience, suggesting that he and Fr. Bruse exchange statues: Fr. Bruse's Fatima statue for his own small statue of St. Elizabeth Ann Seton. Afterward, Fr. Bruse went to the church to celebrate the New Year's vigil Mass (6:00 p.m.).

In the course of their discussion about weeping statues and the like, Fr. Hamilton noticed the small red marks on Fr. Bruse's wrists when he handed him his statue. Father Bruse had not yet mentioned this aspect of his experiences at his parents' house in Stafford. In fact, he knew almost nothing about stigmata wounds or their religious connotation. So, while Fr. Bruse was saying Mass, Fr. Hamilton found an article in the New Catholic Encyclopedia which explained the stigmata phenomenon. He took the book to Fr. Bruse's room and put it on his desk, opened to the right page. As he turned to leave, he noticed the little St. Elizabeth Seton statue, which he had lent to Fr. Bruse, had drops of what appeared to be blood rolling from its eyes and down its cheeks. Shocked, he backed carefully out of the room and returned to his own room. On his dresser was Fr. Bruse's Fatima statue, weeping so profusely that the tears were flowing down the front of his dresser.

On January 2, 1992, Fr. Hamilton phoned the Most Reverend John R. Keating, Bishop of Arlington, to tell him about the events concerning Fr. Bruse. They arranged a meeting for the following day. On January 3, 1992, Fr. Hamilton delivered the Fatima and Seton statues to Bishop Keating. The Seton statue at that time was still stained with the apparent blood, now caked and crusted, which had flowed from its eyes. Regrettably, this material was not analyzed and when Fr. Hamilton retrieved the two statues about a month later on February 5, he washed his Mother Seton statue clean.

Not long after Fr. Hamilton's experience, Marie Pelletier brought her Our Lady of Grace statue to Fr. Bruse to be blessed. Very soon, it also began to weep.

During the next few days, the statue changed some of its coloring as previously described. This statue is now at her home.

During the week of January 12-19, while visiting in the Parish Administrator's home, Fr. Bruse blessed a crucifix belonging to Marie's son, Christopher. Tears immediately began to flow from the Christ figure's eyes.

JANUARY 14-30, 1992

Pinkey first learned of the weeping and stigmata on Tuesday, January 14, 1992, from Mrs. Jackie Ezersky, SEAS' Minister for Religious Education. She immediately telephoned Fr. Bruse and went to see him at the rectory. He told her what had been happening and disclosed that the wrist wounds had recently bled during a 9:00 a.m. weekday Mass. Now sitting in Fr. Bruse's office, Pinkey learned about the stigmata and the weeping statues. While there, she watched a statue of Our Lady of Grace, given to Fr. Bruse by Mrs. Pamela Hood to be blessed, begin to weep profusely. She also observed bleeding from Fr. Bruse's wrist wounds.

My family and I viewed the wrist wounds during our meeting on the 19th of January. Jenny had come home from the University of Virginia in Charlottesville, about a two hour journey, after I had phoned her to report what was happening and invite her to the Sunday afternoon meeting with Fr. Bruse. No statue wept while we were there that day. Nor did Fr. Bruse's stigmata wounds bleed. In fact, they looked as if they *could not* bleed, appearing more like nearly-healed acne than puncture wounds. The small red spots were about the diameter of a pencil, on both sides of the arm, approximately 1" to 2" above the juncture of hand and wrist. (See Figure 2). Father Bruse identified the side wound as being just above his belt. He noted that he had wounds only on the top of his feet, not on the bottom. He told us he had been examined by two physicians, both of whom were baffled by the cause and nature of the bleeding which Fr. Bruse was experiencing from these sites.

Father Bruse told us that these events have perplexed him greatly. He had enjoyed no apparitions nor otherwise received any messages directly from the Virgin Mary or other supernatural being and did not understand the purpose of the manifestations. He speculated that perhaps they were intended to influence certain members and acquaintances of the Bruse family to return to an active faith. Whatever their purpose, he was absolutely convinced of their authenticity as genuine supernatural phenomena.

Figure 1 Photo: Our Lady of Grace statue, like the first to weep in November 1991, weeping on April 29, 1992.

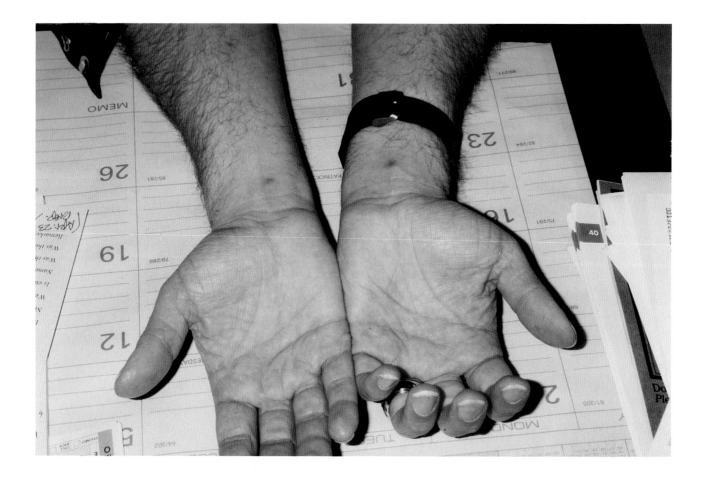

JANUARY 18, 1992

As serendipity would have it, Pinkey and I ended up seated next to Emil and Carol Myskowski at an All-County Band Concert held at Potomac High School this chilly Saturday night. Emil is one of two permanent deacons at SEAS. I wondered if they knew about the weeping statues, but guessed they surely must because of Deacon Emil's position. Wrong guess. During the intermission, I mentioned to them the weeping statues and Fr. Bruse's stigmata wounds. I may as well have told them I had seen little green men dancing on the moon. They mumbled a few polite expressions like "Really?" and "Is that so?" and found other seats after the break. Their disbelief would not last long.

JANUARY 26, 1992

Many other parishioners, especially those who had any official connection with the church, such as members of the Parish Council, were learning about the stigmata and the weeping statues during this time. One of these, Mr. Tom Saunders, was and is a friend of Fr. Bruse. He heard about the weeping statues and Fr. Bruse's stigmata while participating in the 1992 March for Life in Washington (commemorates the infamous January 22, 1973, U.S. Supreme Court decision in *Roe v. Wade)*.

On the 26th of January, Tom took four small Madonna statues to Fr. Bruse to be blessed. All four of them began to weep before Fr. Bruse even had a chance to touch them, much less give them his priestly blessing. Even after Tom returned home, his statues continued to weep for awhile.

Even more remarkable was Tom's experience a couple of weeks later after he had told his wife, Pat, about the phenomena. She gathered up all of her Madonna statues, planters, Christmas creche Mary figures, etc., and sent them in two large plastic bags with Tom to be blessed by Fr. Bruse. Tom estimates he must have had two or three dozen of the little figurines. Each was carefully wrapped in its own towel for protection.

Tom suggested to Fr. Bruse that he just bless them all at once while still in their bags, which he did. When Tom returned home a little while later, and unwrapped the statues, he discovered that every towel which had enfolded a figure was now damp.

Figure 2 Photo: Father Bruse's stigmata wounds in his wrists. Photographed in his office, March 19, 1992.

JANUARY 30, 1992

On Thursday, January 30, 1992, I met with Fr. Bruse alone to discuss the current status of these strange happenings and to ask him to bless two statues of the Blessed Virgin Mary which I had purchased one week earlier at W. Gallery. One of these was a plastic Fatima statue, uncolored except for a uniform pink cast, approximately 15" tall and wearing a small gold crown made of plastic. It is the classic Fatima style with the Madonna, praying hands pressed together beneath her chin, standing atop a cloud with three doves perched on it. My other statue was a "Madonna of the Rose" white ceramic bust, about 8" tall. This statue is white except for five small pink roses placed along Mary's arms plus one held delicately between her praying hands. (See Figure 10).

During my conversation with Fr. Bruse, he related to me that his stigmata wounds remained insignificant in appearance. However, he continued to suffer sharp, intermittent pains at the sites of these wounds, usually once or twice daily, beginning with the wrist wounds and continuing through his feet and, last, to his side. The pattern is always the same. The pains were intense and felt deep-seated to him. He described this pain as analogous to multiple needles driven through his wrists and feet. Although he had not yet experienced any revelations or apparitions to explain the miraculous occurrences, he had begun to experience during these periods of pain a mystical sense of vivid colors which seem to fan out before him. No objects were discernible but the colors were so vivid as to be practically indescribable. Subsequently, he said that even the word "colors" was inadequate to describe what he saw. At these times, he reported he felt as if he had been removed to another dimension, a place of great serenity where he longed to remain.

Father Bruse also related a mystical aspect to the bleeding from his wrist wounds which occurred after the 7:00 a.m. Mass on January 5, 1992. The blood flow appeared not to conform to the normal pull of gravity. When his arms hung down at his sides, the blood did not flow toward the palms but instead flowed around the wrists toward the bottom of his arms, as if they were extended outward. The bleeding was also accompanied by an extraordinary sweet scent, as of flowers.

While discussing with Fr. Bruse some details which I had been uncertain about in the narrative above, he told me that he had another Fatima statue in his bedroom which belonged to his sister, Sue. (See Figure 3). This statue is smaller than the one we saw on January 19, but the colors are very similar. I asked Fr. Bruse if I could see and photograph it. He agreed and brought the statue into his office.

While holding this small statue, I commented to Fr. Bruse on the brightness of the eyes and stated that I did not think they could be glass since the eye cavities were so small. Father Bruse was uncertain himself. In any event, the dark pupils were brightly lit by reflection from an overhead light. While looking at these eyes, I was astonished to see them appear to well up. A moment later, tears flowed out of both eyes of the little statue onto its cheeks. This was not one or two drops but a clearly discernible flow. It is difficult to describe the sequence of emotions which such an event provokes, but in my case they definitely included amazement.

About this time, Fr. Bruse called my attention to the two statues which I had brought to him to be blessed. These he had set on the wooden credenza next to his desk. Both statues were crying profusely! (See Figure 4, a photograph taken five days later). The water had already spread away from the base of the statues. I put my finger into one of the puddles and tasted it. It was clear and fresh-tasting without any hint of contamination with plastic or other materials.

That afternoon, Fr. Bruse was scheduled to undergo a psychological evaluation. This is, I suppose, one of the prices one must pay for the privilege of being God's intermediary in ways which seem inexplicable to the world. The visionaries at Medjugorje in Croatia have been poked, prodded, wired, examined and photographed on numerous occasions.

Father Bruse's encounter with the psychiatrist lasted about 2 1/2 hours. The examination found him normal in his psychiatric make-up with no evidence of hysteria, obsessions or other abnormal mental state.

The most remarkable thing about the experience, however, was the doctor's personal encounter with the same small Fatima statue which I had held that morning. While talking to Fr. Bruse, he glanced over at the statue. Tears were flowing from its eyes. "Your statue is crying," he said simply.

JANUARY 31, 1992

Pinkey reported that for the first time (as far as we know) the statue of the Blessed Virgin Mary, holding the Infant Jesus, inside the church wept. This statue is made of fiberglass and stands about 48 inches high. It is sometimes referred to as "Our Lady of Smiles." The weeping occurred shortly after 4:00 p.m. when Fr. Bruse came over to prepare for a wedding rehearsal to commence later in the hour.

Pinkey told me that Fr. Bruse came downstairs to her office and said, "Pinkey, come upstairs real quick!" He took her over to see the statue. Water was flowing from its eyes. "I tell you," Pinkey commented later, "I thought my legs were going to kick out. I had seen the little ones but there is something about the big one."

Father Bruse told me that when he went over to examine the statue after first noticing that it was crying, the "eyes looked real... human" and tears were flowing out of them. Neither the statue of the Infant Jesus nor Joseph wept. Most members of the staff, along with Ed Glenn, who was at the church checking on the parking lot lighting system, witnessed the weeping.

FEBRUARY 3, 1992

Father Bruse noticed the small "cup" formed by a fold in Mary's dress at the neck of the statue in the church was filled with water. Apparently, this acted as a sort of catch basin for the weeping which occurred last Friday. It may have been residue from a subsequent session, however. If this keeps up, it can't be long before the world will discover what's going on here.

FEBRUARY 4, 1992

I met with Fr. Bruse this morning to go over some of the details of this report and for an update. While I was there, the small Fatima statue wept twice, although the tear flow was less than when I was present on the 30th of January. In addition, the two statues which I had brought the week before wept significant amounts of tears two or three times during the hour and a half interview. (See Figure 4).

I asked Fr. Bruse if he had observed any other phenomena. He told me that the expressions on the Grace and Fatima statues at his parents' house seem to become sadder when the statues weep. Of course, this may just be the subjective effect of seeing tears flow from the eyes of the small figures. On the other hand, others have also reported various degrees of facial animation of inanimate statues.

Father Bruse then related to me an experience which occurred Saturday evening, February 1st. Several priests had come to dinner at the rectory, including Fr. John Dunn, a priest from New Zealand who has assisted our parish with Sunday Masses for the past year or so. After discussing the strange events occurring around Fr. Bruse, the assembled priests examined the small Fatima statue. It began weeping. Father Dunn wiped the tears from the statue's eyes, but they continued to flow. However, Father Dunn later reported that the tearing seemed to stop fairly quickly.

At the conclusion of our meeting, I noted that the small crucifix on Fr. Bruse's office wall had been moved to the left a couple of feet. He explained that

Figure 3 Photo: Father Bruse's sister's Fatima statue weeping in his office on January 30, 1992.

he moved it because it had begun crying and he was concerned since it was directly above an electrical outlet. When I discussed this with Mrs. Pam Hood, subbing for the Parish Administrator that morning, she told me that when the crucifix had wept on the 29th of January, she had brought it out to the work/reception area where her husband, Dean, who happened to be present, also saw the little Christ figure weeping.

FEBRUARY 5, 1992

The church statue of the Madonna with Infant (Our Lady of Smiles) wept again this afternoon. It seems most likely to weep each day between 4 and 5 p.m. When Pinkey saw the statue crying, she called her good friend, Johanna Gregory, who knew about the weeping but had not yet witnessed it.

As Johanna put it, "When I got Pinkey's call, I called Ernie and Jason and we jumped in the car and flew over to the church!"

FEBRUARY 13, 1992

On this cold, snowy Thursday morning, I accompanied John Healy and his mother, Joan, to see Fr. Bruse at the rectory. Mrs. Healy brought a Fatima statue of her own to be blessed by him. After chatting about half an hour, during which time no statue wept, I asked Fr. Bruse if he would mind bringing his sister's Fatima statue (which she had told him to keep) down from his room. He cheerfully complied and not long after his return, the little statue began to weep. Then Joan Healy's statue also began to weep.

FEBRUARY 14, 1992

I came home from work early in order to help Pinkey get ready for the One-act Play presentation before a parish audience this evening. I went upstairs in the church about 4:25 p.m. and saw Father Bruse and Jackie Ezersky standing over by the Madonna with Infant (Our Lady of Smiles) statue. They had taken it down from its pedestal and were peering at it. When I went over to see what was going on, I saw the statue had been weeping. The actual tearing had ended, but there was still water in the eyes.

Figure 4 Photo: *Close-up of Carneys' Fatima statue weeping in Fr. Bruse's office on February 4, 1992.*

FEBRUARY 15, 1992

Pinkey and I hosted a dinner party tonight for Fr. Bruse, Fr. John Dunn, Johanna and Ernie Gregory, and Pam Hood. Father Bruse was not feeling well. He told Pinkey that his stigmata wounds, especially the wrists, were paining him very much. He also said he was experiencing visions.

About 9:30 p.m., Pinkey went out to the kitchen and noticed what appeared to be water on top of the antique desk in the family room where the Our Lady of Fatima statue (Fig. 4) stands. The statue was weeping! All members of the dinner party saw this, as it continued for about ten minutes after we discovered it.

FEBRUARY 18, 1992

Father Bruse celebrated Mass at the main church of Our Lady of Angels this morning. While at the altar, he glanced toward the back of the church where the great round stained glass window image of Our Lady of Angels looked down on the children, teachers and parishioners assembled for daily Mass. "Tears" were flowing from the corners of the Madonna's eyes in a pronounced stream. Since the congregation faces away from the window, there may have been no one else who noticed this.

Tom Saunders talked to Fr. Bruse about this occasion. "As he was standing there, in the middle of the Mass, and he looked up, there was water pouring down that window! He said he didn't say a word. He just finished the Mass and got out of there!"

FEBRUARY 22, 1992

SEAS' annual Senior Catholic Youth Ministry (SR CYM) Spaghetti Dinner was held tonight. Father Bruse left early when his stigmata wounds began to pain him severely. They also bled later. This was the first time in about 10-14 days that they had bled, although the pains of the wounds have been regularly experienced about once or twice daily. These are the times when his visions occur.

FEBRUARY 23, 1992

Carol Myskowski, wife of Deacon Emil Myskowski, brought four statues of the Blessed Virgin Mary to the rectory for Fr. Bruse to bless. There were two additional ones which she left home, one of which, a small, white ceramic statue of Mary holding the Infant Jesus, was broken in two and missing its halo.

All four of the statues wept while Carol was present in Fr. Bruse's office. She took them home with her later that Sunday afternoon and placed them, together with the two broken statues, on her dining room table while she and her husband met with a young couple about their wedding plans. A couple of hours later, she noticed the ceramic statue was no longer in two pieces but was now fused together. The crack between the two pieces is still visible in an arch along the shoulder line, but only barely so. Carol reports that no member of her family repaired the statue and there was no other person who could have done so. It appears, therefore, to be a case similar to the inexplicable coloring of other Madonna statues.

I examined the small statue closely on the evening of February 26th. There was no evidence of gluing or other means of repairing the break. The statue is hollow and the inside can be viewed from a hole in the bottom. The two halves are put together precisely correctly, although there is a small chip missing near the bottom curve of the break. I also noticed that the crack would separate very slightly near the shoulder. This came to my attention when I heard a slight "click" while examining the statue. The rest of the crack seemed firm. The broken-off halo is still missing.

FEBRUARY 25, 1992

This evening, Fr. Bruse accompanied Jackie Ezersky to St. Columba's Catholic Church in Oxon Hill, MD. Mrs. Ezersky was to give a talk there at 7 p.m. on Children's Liturgy of the Word. Sue Farr, Father Bruse's sister, is the Assistant Director of CCD at St. Columba. Shortly after their arrival, water began to flow from the corner of the eye of a life-sized etched glass image of the Blessed Virgin Mary inside the church. This was observed by Fr. Bruse and Mrs. Ezersky, who jokingly told Fr. Bruse, "I told you to keep your hands in your pockets!"[1] A stain or a discoloration of some sort from that weeping and subsequent ones is still visible on the glass. (See Figure 5).

---

[1]Mrs. Ezersky's attitude has offended some people who believe that the sight of an image of the Blessed Virgin Mary appearing to weep should not be the subject of levity. This is probably true but such experiences produce different effects in different people, like those who feel a compulsion to laugh at funerals. Other people, even regular church-goers, have simply refused to accept the testimony of their own eyes and the objective evidence of the camera and insist that there must be some natural explanation for the crying. These reactions are a reminder that faith is a gift and many people have a great struggle to fully accept the reality of the supernatural world.

During this visit, Fr. Bruse had a profound mystical experience similar in nature but more extensive in degree than ones he had been having earlier. He did not, however, see an apparition or receive any message explaining the significance of the weeping, etc., which was occurring through him.

I asked Fr. Bruse about the physical reaction of the stigmata wounds when they bleed. He said they do not literally become an open wound or even change shape. Blood just begins to ooze out of the reddened areas on his body which mark the approximate locations of the wounds of Christ. Not all of the sites bleed, either, at least not on all occasions. Normally, he said, the blood flow is minor but sometimes it is very heavy.

FEBRUARY 26, 1992

I brought a very old (circa 1915) Hummel porcelain statue of the Blessed Virgin Mary to Fr. Bruse to be blessed. The statue belongs to Fr. Chuck McCoart, the Diocesan Youth Director. It was handed down to him from his grandmother. After its blessing, the statue did begin to weep. At the time, there were several other statues present which various parishioners had brought in to be blessed. For awhile, six little statues were quietly weeping together. (See Figure 6).

I returned to the rectory this evening to photograph Carol Myskowski's mysteriously fused statue. There were numerous statues present, including three new Our Lady of Grace statues which Fr. Bruse had received that day from W. Gallery. One of these is shown in Figure 1. No statue wept during this visit. This is significant only because it reveals that tearing is not constant, nor does it always occur when visitors appear. It is perhaps noteworthy, however, that Fr. Bruse's personal Fatima statue (see Figure 3) was not present. In all my recent visits to the rectory, this beautiful little statue with the lifelike, melancholy eyes has never failed to weep. And that always seems to precipitate tears from any other Madonna statues which may be present.

While discussing these latest phenomena, Fr. Bruse and Marie Pelletier reported that they had noticed a lovely sweet fragrance when his Fatima statue had wept in his room a couple of days earlier. This phenomenon is fairly infrequent, although a few other persons have also reported experiencing an extraordinarily delightful fragrance, often described as the smell of roses.

A small Madonna statue belonging to Mrs. Isobel Milligan, SEAS' Coordinator of Confirmation and Middle School, has been colored, presumably by the same source which has produced the other statue colorations. In this case, Mrs. Milligan's statue had a white gown with blue mantle. The gown is now a golden

Figure 5 Photo: *Etched glass image of the Virgin Mary with tear stains at Saint Columba's Church, May 27, 1992.*

yellow. This occurred after she had left the statue with Fr. Bruse. Her statue is the fourth one from the left in Figure 6.

FEBRUARY 28, 1992

Several catechists and staff members of SEAS attended the East Coast Conference for Religious Educators which began today at the Omni Shoreham Hotel in Washington, D.C. Father Bruse also attended. During one of the program breaks, he strolled through the religious vendors' display area, stopping at the W. Gallery booth. Marie Pelletier and Isobel Milligan accompanied him. In addition to a variety of literature, W. Gallery also had a few crucifixes and other articles hanging on a four-sided, free-standing display pillar. As Father Bruse stood before it, one of the crucifixes began to weep. Upon seeing this, Marie removed the crucifix from the display, wiped it dry, and purchased it. Only the one crucifix wept. No one else appeared to notice the water flowing from the metal eyes of the Christ figure.

Subsequently, the crucifix continued to weep inside its tissue paper wrapping and box, so much so that within two hours the paper was thoroughly drenched and the bottom of the box was becoming weakened by the collection of water there. Pinkey and I gave Fr. Bruse and Marie a ride home from the conference that afternoon. During the trip, we checked the crucifix a couple of times. Each time it had water drops on its chest.

Perhaps the most remarkable thing about this experience, however, occurred about five minutes from Lake Ridge when Fr. Bruse picked up the crucifix and was holding it cradled in his left hand with his right fingers resting on its chest. He felt a strong energy flow from the crucifix, likened by him to an electric current, and discovered he could not remove his fingers. This continued until we arrived at the rectory some 10-15 minutes later.

MARCH 2, 1992

Father Hamilton and Father Bruse met with Bishop Keating at the Chancery today. Monsignor William Reinecke, the Diocesan Chancellor, was also present. Both prelates had Madonna statues. Bishop Keating had two in his office and Monsignor Reinecke brought one of his own. In addition, Fr. Bruse had brought his little Fatima statue with him. All the statues wept. Reportedly, this has convinced Bishop Keating that the weeping is a genuine phenomenon and should be so treated. However, his counsel was to continue observation, pray, and await some spiritual revelation or guidance to shed light upon the meaning of these

Figure 6 Photo: Six statues of Our Blessed Mother weeping in Fr. Bruse's office on February 26, 1992.

occurrences and what our response should be. He stated that the Church does not investigate mere physical phenomena but, rather, requires an alleged communication from God before determining whether the event is worthy of belief by the faithful.

After leaving the bishop's office, Fathers Hamilton and Bruse passed a crucifix hanging on the wall. Father Bruse touched it briefly, whereupon tears began flowing from the Christ figure's eyes. Father Hamilton suggested to two secretaries in a nearby office that they might want to take a look at the crucifix, but he did not remain to observe their reaction.

Jackie Ezersky showed me her rosary today. This blue crystal rosary has small blue squares which separate the decades. Two of these squares changed in color from blue to green after the rosary was blessed by Fr. Bruse. [See page 63 for a discussion of some of the rosary color changes which occurred during this period.]

MARCH 3, 1992

Pinkey reported that the Madonna with Infant statue in the church wept this afternoon. Father Bruse removed it from its pedestal and put it in the light so Pinkey could photograph it. "When Father Jim picked up the statue to put it back on its pedestal, its tears began to flow even more heavily," Pinkey noted. Far more incredible to her, she thought she saw the eyes of the statue move, especially when Fr. Bruse was gently moving it. She mentioned this, somewhat incredulously, to him.

He said, "That's okay, Pinkey. I have seen it."

Three of the pictures which she took on this occasion are at Figures 7, 8 and 9.

Later on, Tom Saunders would tell me of some of the weepings of this statue which he witnessed. "Sometimes that statue just... it just poured out! I've actually seen it splashing off the arm of the Child. Other times, it's just been a few drops, or wet around the eyes, or whatever."

The volume of calls from parishioners and persons outside the parish is accelerating.

The CBS affiliate here, WUSA Channel 9, "Eyewitness News," called this evening to inquire about the happenings. Father Bruse took the call and referred them to Fr. Hamilton but requested they wait until after Ash Wednesday (tomorrow) to call him.

Figures 7, 8, & 9 Photos: Madonna with Infant (Our Lady of Smiles) statue in St. Elizabeth Seton Church weeping on March 3, 1992.

Figure 7

Figure 8

MARCH 4, 1992
Ash Wednesday

Father Hamilton told me this morning that he had learned at the Chancery on Monday that there are 155 cases of reported apparitions, weepings and other alleged supernatural occurrences pending right now in the United States.

The Madonna with Infant statue was reported to weep at each of the Ash Wednesday Masses celebrated by Fr. Bruse. A large number of people witnessed these sessions.

Libby Lawler, a SEAS parishioner and Kindergarten teacher at Aquinas School, took her two sons, Michael and Joey to the 4:30 p.m. children's liturgy.

After the Mass, they went up to examine the Our Lady of Smiles statue and found it crying. "It was coming right down her face, right down the front of her robe, settling at her feet."

Linda Christie describes what she saw at the 7 p.m. Mass:

> "On Thursday, after school I had a real desire to go by SEAS, which I did. Nobody was in the church when I arrived a little before 4. I went up to the statue on the right side of the church and really studied it. She was bone dry. I even touched the table at the base and it was dry. We decided to attend the 7PM Mass and arrived about ten minutes early. Sandy Dunlap was looking at the statue with another lady when we arrived. It was obvious they were seeing something. Sandy then brought Rita Cairns up to the statue and I heard Rita say 'Oh my God!' I asked Jack [Linda's husband] if he wanted to go over and see, which we did as quietly as we could. The statue now looked just like Libby [Lawler] had described she had looked on Ash Wednesday afternoon: her eyes were filled with 'tears', there were splashes on what would be the front of her dress, and there was a puddle that was large enough for me to easily put two fingers in it (4 inches in diameter I would say) and bless myself."

MARCH 6, 1992

Channel 9's "Eyewitness News" broadcast the first media report of the "Seton Miracles" tonight at 11:00 p.m. It was a good, well-balanced report with some historical data about Padre Pio and Theresa Neumann (20th Century stigmatics) and St. Francis of Assisi. They even managed to capture two of the Fatima statues in Fr. Bruse's office weeping on camera.

MARCH 7, 1992

We began to get a flavor today of what might be coming. Late in the afternoon, when the church was locked up because the staff had gone home, as Pinkey herself was leaving the church, she saw a man kneeling on the sidewalk before the closed front doors, praying the rosary. He seemed oblivious to the rain which pelted down upon him. Pinkey suggested he move under the roof overhang but he insisted he preferred to be where he was. She asked him why he was praying the rosary under such circumstances and he replied, "I just wanted to be close to her." Pinkey then decided to stay a little longer and invited the man inside the church to see the Madonna with Infant statue. It was not weeping at the time, but the man prayed for awhile before the statue and later lay prone on the stairs before the crucifix above the altar and began to confess his sins out loud. Pinkey waited in the back of the church, out of earshot, and let him out of the church when he was finished.

This afternoon, Fr. Bruse, Marie Pelletier and Pam Hood all visited Rachel Pevarnik at Fairfax Hospital. The little two-year old girl began her chemotherapy treatments today. Her parents, Joe and Julie, and grandparents were with her. Marie brought Rachel a small, ceramic Our Lady of Grace statue, about 7" tall. The statue was new and still wrapped in tissue in its box. Marie handed it to Fr. Bruse for his blessing. Joe describes what happened next:

> "The statue lay in his hands, the left one below the right one. He closed his eyes and went into deep prayer. Within a few seconds tears began flowing like a stream of water from the eyes of the statue. Suddenly, the entire statue was wet as were Father Jim's hands. At this point, Rachel's mother, who was lying next to Rachel in the bed, touched her hands with the statue, thus absorbing the tears onto them and then rubbed her hands along Rachel's leg, her abdomen and forehead. We all looked in amazement. We were quiet. We could not believe our eyes. This indeed was a miracle."

MARCH 9, 1992

The crowds have arrived! "Pilgrims," parishioners who did not know about the phenomena before, and the press have been flocking to the church in droves. Yesterday's Masses were all packed, into the vestibule. The votive candle displays are blazing away in constant flame and require frequent replacement throughout the day. Pinkey reports that all of the plastic rosaries which had been hanging by the front door have disappeared. She brought her own pictures of weeping statues home after discovering a large number of children and a few adults in her office looking at them yesterday. The phones are ringing off the hook, with many calls coming from out-of-state, often asking for directions to the church. UPI was on the scene today. Several TV stations sent cameras yesterday, but Fr. Bruse celebrated only the 9:30 a.m. Mass at SEAS. His 11:00 a.m. Mass was at Rockledge Elementary School, where there are no statues.

There were pilgrims outside the church's front doors about 9:00 p.m. last night, kneeling to pray the rosary. Today, people have continued the practice. More than 100 people stayed for the rosary following the 9:00 a.m. Mass this morning. Reportedly, the Madonna with Infant statue wept then.

All of the staff are at least somewhat frazzled by the tremendous public response to the news reports. Both *The Washington Post* and the *Potomac News* ran articles today. Father Bruse appears to be holding up well, calmly extending his blessing to all who request it. One woman told him that she also was a stigmatic, albeit an "inner one" (the wounds are not visible). She declared she was having visions and asked Fr. Bruse to bless her to keep the devil away. She gave him a rosary with white beads to bless, which he did. He had no sooner handed it back to her when she exclaimed that her rosary had turned blue. Father Bruse described the color of the rosary as a "creamy blue" but said that he did not actually see it change color and could not refute the possibility that the woman had merely switched rosaries after he handed it back to her.

The church is a zoo! It is even difficult to find a parking place and the staff can hardly get its work done between answering phones and personal queries about Fr. Bruse and weeping statues. Finally, in frustration, Pinkey left to try to find someplace more quiet to work. On her way out, Fr. Bruse remarked plaintively, "Surely it won't be like this every day!?"

MARCH 12, 1992

Father Hamilton and Fr. Bruse conducted a press conference in the church at 11:00 a.m. this morning. This would be the first and last one to be offered on this subject, according to Fr. Hamilton. About 100 media/press personnel showed up, including all of the local TV affiliates. Mr. Chris Gordon, a weekend anchorman for Channel 9, was the only relatively prominent media figure present.

Marie Pelletier introduced the conference. Father Bruse then offered a few remarks. He was followed by Fr. Hamilton who fielded questions for about half an hour. The tone of the conference was definitely tilted toward downplaying the events, with Fr. Hamilton reporting the stigmata had disappeared and referring at one point to the large Madonna with Infant statue as "producing water" instead of weeping. The statue did not weep for the press this day, although a couple of reporters asked Fr. Bruse to touch the statue to see if it would begin weeping. He declined. Later that day, around 4:30 p.m., during the period when the church was closed, the statue did weep and copiously.

Pinkey remarked later, "I've never seen the statue weep so much."

There were many of us who would have liked to mingle our own tears with Our Lady's that sad afternoon.

MARCH 17, 1992
ST. PATRICK'S DAY

This day would turn out to be one of the most momentous days in the story of weeping statues and Fr. Bruse. It began with Fr. Bruse saying the 11:00 a.m. Mass at Our Lady of Angels for the children of Aquinas School. Near the end of the service, he noticed several persons kind of scurrying around at the back of the nave and just inside the vestibule. After Mass was over, he learned that the lifesize wooden statue of Our Lady in the vestibule of the church had begun to shed tears. This weeping continued in full view of the children and adults who attended Mass or otherwise happened to be present. Father Paul Burns, pastor of Our Lady of Angels, was called to the church and he, too, viewed the weeping phenomenon. A week later, he wrote a letter to the entire parish and included it in the March 29th Sunday bulletin. (See Appendix B). Sister Mary Evelyn Potts, Principal of Aquinas School, sent a letter home with all the students informing their parents of what had happened and assuring them it was not simply a matter of a runaway childhood imagination.

Linda Christie, who teaches sixth grade at Aquinas School, stated later in her own fascinating report that some students claimed to see the concrete Madonna statue, which stands outside the school entrance, opening and closing her eyes. "I really think this was probably the result of over-active imagination, but I went out and I tell you I would not swear that she wasn't doing that." She polled her class that afternoon about this truly fantastic claim. "How many of you really believe you saw her eyes open and close?" she asked. Nearly all hands went up. Merely the power of suggestion? Read on.

Marcia (pronounced "Mar-see") Grattan is a science teacher at Aquinas School. On this day, when she was passing near the concrete Madonna statue, the Physical Education teacher at Aquinas called urgently to her to come and see the statue. She walked over to see what he wanted. "He just kept saying,'They're usually down, they're usually halfway closed!'" She followed his gaze to the eyes of the statue. "They were open! Almost immediately after that," Marcia said, "Sister and Fr. Jim came walking out of the school building. I'm waving them over. Father Jim went right up to it, and Sister did, and we went back, and further back, and close up, and further back." But the eyes remained open.

The P.E. teacher reported that the eyes were beginning to close slightly before Marcia and the others arrived. By the time another friend of Marcia's walked up, the eyes had returned to their normal half-lidded position. "Since then," Marcia says, "many times I have tried to stand at every possible distance and angle in front of that statue and I don't care where you are, that statue's eyes are half closed. They are not wide open. [But] those eyes WERE open. They were open!"

Late that afternoon, Fr. Bruse came to our house for dinner. He had to leave about 6:00 p.m. because he was saying the evening Mass and then going to a Knights of Columbus meeting. Other guests were Fr. Chuck McCoart (Diocesan Youth Director); Fr. Hamilton; my nieces, Ashley and Nicole Barrett; and Elaine Heath, a college friend of Jenny's. Of course, Jenny, Jay, Pinkey and I were also present. We had a few religious articles that we wanted Fr. Bruse to bless, including statues of the Blessed Virgin Mary, rosaries and a small bottle of holy water. All of these items were placed on top of the antique hideaway desk in our family room.

Father Bruse arrived about 4:00 p.m., followed shortly thereafter by Fr. McCoart. The three of us went downstairs to talk. Pinkey stayed in the kitchen to prepare the meal. Not long after, Fr. Hamilton and then Ashley and Nicole arrived. Elaine had come in earlier in the afternoon. Pinkey called us up for dinner about 4:45 p.m. As we converged in the family room, someone noticed that some of the statues were weeping. These included our pink Fatima statue (Figure 4), Elaine's Our Lady of Grace with Roses, and the new porcelain Madonna statue which I had just purchased for Jenny the day before from the Paschal Lamb, a religious goods store.

After observing this for a few minutes, I went into the living room where Pinkey and I were keeping our Touch of Rose Madonna bust on a glass-enclosed shelf in a teak wall unit. This statue was also weeping! The water had already collected around and under the base. (See Figure 10). After photographing the statue, I removed it from the cabinet and handed it to Jenny. She told me later that as she and Elaine held the small figure, tears continued to emerge from the eyes and roll down the Madonna's face.

Father McCoart's Hummel statue, which had wept in Fr. Bruse's office a little over two weeks ago, was resting on top of an antique sewing machine across the room from the Madonna bust. But it did not weep at this time.

Although they did not say so, I believe my two nieces, Ashley and Nicole, were quite disappointed that their Madonna statues had not shed any tears. Actually, this feeling was common to many people who hoped to see a statue weep but did not. There is a little nagging fear that perhaps the Blessed Mother has looked into our souls and discovered there just how unworthy we really are—much too unworthy to be permitted to view a miraculous suspension of the laws of science. But, in actuality, there appears not to have been any such standard of merit applied to the instances of weeping which occurred at SEAS. I am living proof of that.

After this initial display of the statues weeping had ended, we split up to eat. Father Bruse sat with the four young ladies in the kitchen and Fathers Hamilton and McCoart sat with Pinkey, Jay and me in the dining room. At this time, too, Fr. Bruse blessed all of the statues on the desk, making a small sign of the cross over them. About 5:40 p.m., Fr. Bruse left for the rectory. As he did so, he told Pinkey that he sensed Ashley and Nicole were distressed that their statues had not wept. He told Pinkey to check them again later because sometimes the weeping would begin after he had left.

Perhaps twenty minutes later, someone noticed that the statues were, indeed, weeping. This time only the statues on the left side of the desk were crying. These included the two from my nieces and a small, plain white ceramic one from Elaine. In addition, there may have been some tearing from one of the rosaries inside a small cloth case. Certainly, later in the evening this case was noticeably wet. Further, two of the rosaries which were not in cases had drops of water near their crucifixes. The exact origin of this water could not be determined.

The Madonna bust in the glass case and Father McCoart's Hummel Madonna, both of which were still in the living room, did not weep at this time. The weeping continued for perhaps 10-15 minutes.

After dinner, we adjourned to the rec room downstairs to continue our conversation. I spent some time talking to the Barrett girls about religion. I do not recall when Fr. Hamilton left, but sometime after that, Pinkey went upstairs to the kitchen. When she did so, she said she saw out of the corner of her eye what looked like a kind of glow in the corner where the desk was located. She went

Figure 9.

Figure 9

over to it and found several of the Madonna statues were weeping again. Water had collected in the holy water basin which formed the base of one of the Barretts' little statues. Pinkey called us up and we all viewed this latest event. After a few minutes, I went out to the living room and brought Fr. McCoart's Hummel Madonna into the family room and placed it with the others on the desk top. At this point, his was the only Madonna statue which had not wept that evening. We then returned downstairs and resumed our conversation.

About 11:30 p.m., Ashley and Nicole decided to depart, taking their two Madonna statues and the rosary in the cloth case with them. Perhaps half an hour later, Fr. McCoart also prepared to leave. When we came upstairs to the family room to get the Hummel Madonna for him to take with him, we found it weeping profusely! After observing this for a few minutes, he wrapped the statue in the green hand towel Pinkey had borrowed to transport it when she first received it from him. A few days later, he told Pinkey that the towel was soaking wet by the time he arrived back at the St. Mary of Sorrows rectory in Springfield that night, indicating the statue continued to weep during his trip home.

At around 1:00 a.m., Elaine and Jenny decided to retire for the evening and left Pinkey and me chatting downstairs. A few moments later, Elaine came dashing down the stairs and exclaimed excitedly that the statues were weeping again. I do not recall whether the Fatima statue wept at this time, but all the others did. In addition, there were drops of water near the rosary crucifixes. When I checked on the Madonna bust in the wall unit, it was once again dry. I decided to move it to the top of the desk, where there was now plenty of room since Elaine had removed her statue to be with her in our guest room. Pinkey and I then decided to go to bed ourselves.

After beginning my preparations for bed, I came down to the family room to see what was keeping Pinkey. I found her on her knees before the desk, praying silently. I went over to join her and saw that the Madonna bust was now weeping also, but by itself. It had formed the most lovely tear, gathered like a small, round crystal on her right cheek. This was the sixth, and presumably last, time this evening that one or more of the statues/crucifixes wept.

Two observations on this night's wondrous events. First, although there was considerable water at various times on the top and front of the desk, there was no trace of stain or residue left after the "tears" had evaporated, which seemed to occur fairly rapidly. This was also true of the tear water in the teak wall unit, a type of wood which is notoriously susceptible to water stains. Second, Ashley later told me that there was the most lovely scent of roses in her room that night. Since she had no flowers nor other natural explanation for this odor, it seems likely that the scent was produced from the tear water still in the basin of the little Madonna

Figure 10 Photo: *Touch of Rose Madonna statue weeping inside glass cabinet, moved back to show water collected at the base.*

holy water font. Several other persons have reported the scent of roses, or incense, when these weepings have occurred. I, myself, have not experienced this phenomenon. Even more awesome, of course, is the possibility that the fragrance indicates the supernatural presence of the Blessed Virgin Mary herself. Some of the situations described in this book suggest that.

While some of this was transpiring at our residence, Fr. Bruse returned to SEAS, said Mass, and went on to the Knights of Columbus meeting in the basement of the church. Tom Saunders, a Fourth Degree Knight like Fr. Bruse, was at the meeting that night and took a photo which would achieve worldwide attention.

Fran Perotti brought two fairly large Madonna statues to the meeting. One was a representation of Our Lady of Medjugorje. The other was an Our Lady of Lourdes statue. Both were between two and three feet tall. They were kept in the sacristy until Fr. Bruse finished saying the evening Mass.

After Mass, Fr. Bruse carried the Our Lady of Lourdes statue, cradled in his arms, downstairs to the meeting area. As Tom put it, the statue "left a trail of water right across the vestibule and down the steps... I mean you could walk behind him and think someone with a cup of water just dribbled it across the hall!"

Both statues were placed on a table while the Knights conducted their meeting. Both wept profusely. Tom had brought his camera that night, for reasons which he didn't fully appreciate but which he now believes were related to the photograph he was about to take. "I did not know if anything was going to come out," he said, although he is an accomplished amateur photographer. He was not sure the tears would show up on film. Maybe they would be like an apparition, he thought, real to the viewer but not visible to anyone else. In any event, the picture which Tom took of the statue of Our Lady of Medjugorje weeping is at Figure 11. "That picture has been around the world," notes Tom, obviously pleased that his picture has been so well-received. "It's been all over Europe and Asia, down in Central and South America; it's been to Canada."

Tom later would note that these supernatural events during this time seemed to happen in waves. "Some days you could really feel it and other days it just wasn't there." The "waves" were towering on this unforgettable St. Patrick's Day, 1992.

MARCH 19, 1992

Father Bruse told me that he has noticed a beautiful fragrance of roses emanating from the small Fatima statue's tears, especially after they have been

Figure 11 Photo: Our Lady of Medjugorje statue weeping at SEAS's Knights of Columbus meeting March 17, 1992.

sitting awhile. This scent is also present at his mother's house, most particularly from a small jar of the tear water which she has accumulated and saves from evaporation by enclosing it.

When I entered his office I immediately noticed a beautiful Fatima statue, about 25 inches high, standing on a small table across from his desk. The statue has hands clasped in prayer but there is no rosary which is part of the statue. Father Bruse refers to it as a "Type 3" Fatima statue. The figure began to weep almost as soon as Fr. Bruse entered his office. Tear drops can be seen emerging from both eyes in the photo at Figure 12.

My daughter, Jenny, gave me a tiny sterling silver crucifix, about one inch long, on a silver chain to be blessed by Fr. Bruse. I requested he do so as we were concluding this interview. He took the crucifix into his left hand, placed his right hand over the top as if he were tenderly holding an egg, and offered a silent blessing of about 5-10 seconds. When he removed his right hand, his cupped left hand holding the crucifix was filled with water! It still provokes in me the most wonderful feeling of awe and reverence. It is often hard to force myself to get out the camera and try to preserve the moment for posterity.

During this interview, I asked Fr. Bruse how he interpreted all of these remarkable phenomena. He replied, "Christ is giving us a sign, telling us it is 100% real and saying, 'Now, what are you going to do about it?'"

MARCH 20, 1992

Karen Muller, a parishioner and member of the choir, reported that the Madonna with Infant statue wept for forty minutes before the daily 9:00 a.m. Mass. Afterwards, a man asked Fr. Bruse to bless his statue of the Sacred Heart of Jesus. Fr. Bruse did so and the statue immediately began to weep.

MARCH 23, 1992

Virginia Allen, visiting from Maine, noticed a strong scent of roses in church after Mass, as well as out in the parking lot. She overheard two or three parishioners also commenting about a scent of roses in the air.

MARCH 24, 1992

This is Father's Bruse's week to say daily Mass. Throngs of people attend and wait patiently afterwards for his blessing. Pinkey remembers this particular Tuesday vividly:

Figure 12 Photo: Fatima statue, about 25 inches high, weeping in Fr. Bruse's office on March 19, 1992.

"I had left my office, running a little late, to hurry over to a 10:00 a.m. staff meeting at the rectory. As I climbed the stairs toward the church vestibule, I could hear lots of voices. I wondered what was going on; Mass would have ended a half hour ago. As I emerged from the stairwell I saw Fr. Jim in the middle of a large group of people holding statues, waiting for him to bless them. Several of the statues began to cry before Fr. Jim touched them.

Outside, I was amazed to see a long line of people waiting to see Fr. Jim. As I walked along toward the rectory, I was even more amazed to see that some of the statues which people were holding were already weeping. These statues were all sizes and styles—some just 3-4 inches, others as big as four feet high! The people whose statues were weeping were in a state of awe. Even the people whose statues were not weeping were awestruck by the ones that were. Many people seemed deeply moved."

MARCH 27, 1992

Father Bruse officiated today at a funeral at his sister's parish (Saint Columba in Oxon Hill, MD). During the course of the funeral, two Madonna statues, a crucifix and the etched glass image of the Blessed Virgin Mary (see Figure 5) wept.

MARCH 30, 1992

The Lenten/Easter communal penance service was held tonight. Father Bruse was one of the confessors in attendance. The church was very crowded, "packed," according to Marcia Grattan, who was seated near the front of the church. "At one point, for a very short time, thirty seconds at the most, I smelled the most beautiful floral smell. There was a lady in front of me and I thought, ooooh, it must be her perfume." At the time, Marcia did not wonder why the scent was so sudden, so strong and so brief if it were coming from another person's perfume. "I just smelled a BEAUTIFUL floral odor for a very short period of time," she says.

The next day, another teacher at Aquinas School, Sharon Cyphers, came up to her and said, "Hey, Marcia. Did you smell that pretty flower... that rose smell?"

Marcia reacted with shock. "I almost lost it right there in the school. She said, 'Just for a real short period of time; it just came into the room?'" Sharon had been sitting near the back of the church, at least ten rows behind Marcia.

Two days later, Marcia told Fr. Bruse about the experience and he confided that several people had been coming up to him and telling him about this experience. "He said, 'That's been going on now for a couple of weeks.'"

MARCH 31, 1992

Father Bruse went to Our Lady of Angels Church today to participate in a communal penance service for the third, fifth and sixth grades. Linda Christie and Marcia Grattan were two of the teachers present. They saw the wooden statue of the Blessed Virgin weeping... but there was no Fr. Bruse. In fact, however, he was there. He simply had not entered the church yet. As Marcia noted, "He had just driven into the parking lot and that statue had started to cry!"

APRIL 1, 1992

Father Bruse said that he is experiencing a very pronounced fragrance of roses in his room at the rectory—when there are no flowers there.

APRIL 3, 1992

Pinkey reported that Fr. Bruse's stigmata wounds began to bleed again today.

APRIL 5, 1992

Fran and Jennifer Perotti described an amazing series of events which happened this day. It began with Fran and Jennifer taking Fr. Bruse to dinner at the house of Fran's brother, Bob Perotti, in Manassas. The three of them were in the Perotti's car heading up Davis Ford Road. Father Bruse was seated in the back next to a replica of the Vatican's Pieta statue wrapped in a towel. On the way, Fr. Bruse removed the towel, blessed the statue, and handed it to Jennifer. Immediately, tears began to flow from the eyes of the Virgin Mary holding the figure of her prostrate, crucified son.

"He handed me the statue and it's crying, I mean pouring!" exclaimed Jennifer. "The tears were coming so heavily they soaked my skirt."

Jennifer describes what happened next: "I'm looking at the statue and the eyes are closed. She's [the Pieta is a statue by Michelangelo, portraying the Blessed Virgin Mary holding the body of her crucified son] holding Jesus in her arms. While I'm looking at it and the tears are pouring down, she opened her eyes and she looked right at me! I couldn't believe what I was seeing! So, I'm looking at marble eyes open, marble eyes full of tears, looking right into my eyes. I got so upset, I started screaming: 'She's looking at me, she opened her eyes!' Fran almost ran off the road. Fr. Jim's sitting in the back seat, very calm, saying, 'It's okay, I understand. I know. I know.'"

When Jennifer looked back at the statue, the eyes of the Virgin were closed again.

Fran and Jennifer were the first guests to arrive at his brother's house. On a table inside was a flower arrangement with a small statue of Our Lady in it. As soon as Fr. Bruse walked in, this little statue began to weep. There was a white ceramic statue resting in a china cabinet. It, too, began to cry. As they looked around, every statue of the Blessed Virgin Mary which they could see was shedding tears.

Up until this time, Bob Perotti had been somewhat skeptical about the reports of weeping statues, querying Fran as to whether he was certain that the moisture was not being caused by some odd humidity condition in the church. Bob's skepticism went out the door this day. Altogether, some twelve representations of the Blessed Mother wept this incredible afternoon, including a wooden icon of her which another guest had obtained in Germany.

Later in the afternoon, Jennifer Perotti was admiring a two-foot Fatima statue which was weeping. A young friend (in his early twenties) of the family picked the statue up to examine it more closely. When he did so, he suddenly froze. Jennifer could hardly move herself. She stared at the statue and said to Joe: "Are you seeing what I'm seeing?"

"Yes, ma'am," came the reply.

What they were seeing was the eyes of the statue moving back and forth. "He [Joe] could hardly talk, he was so in awe," said Jennifer. "He was converted. He's never been the same." Later, when Jennifer described these incidents to Fr. Bruse's mother, she acknowledged but did not describe similar experiences.

APRIL 7, 1992

Father Bruse offered the daily Mass for the Aquinas school children at Our Lady of Angels today. One new Fatima statue belonging to the school's principal, Sister Mary Evelyn, wept while he was carrying it from the church to her office in the school building. He had blessed it in the sacristy. A photographer from the *Potomac News* was present and captured this weeping statue on film.

That afternoon, Father Bruse met with the Aquinas faculty and reviewed his experiences with all the phenomena since the beginning. He told them that ten Blessed Mother statues (seven Our Lady of Fatima and three Our Lady of Grace) had displayed color changes. He noted the color changes were not just on the surface but seemed to emanate from the very material itself. He also reported that the tear water from two statues had been analyzed. One result showed the properties of human tears (saline, etc.). The other had no properties whatsoever (no chlorine or other mineral content) but was simply pure H_2O.

At the end of his talk, Fr. Bruse blessed all the statues, rosaries, pictures, crucifixes, and other items which the people had brought. Shortly afterward, he carried one of the little statues downstairs for the praying of the rosary. By the bottom of the stairs, the statue was crying and continued to weep for approximately a half hour.

APRIL 10, 1992

Father Bruse's stigmata wounds began to bleed tonight as soon as the Senior CYM's Living Stations (enactment of the Stations of the Cross) presentation began. Pinkey witnessed the bleeding and got some tissues for him to use to absorb the blood. He told Pinkey that he has been having pains at the wound sites once or twice a day throughout Lent. With Holy Week nearly here, many of us are wondering if Fr. Bruse will have some dramatic spiritual experience in connection with Good Friday.

Carol Marino noticed a very strong scent of roses during the 9:00 a.m. daily Mass. Someone had brought a traveling Our Lady of Medjugorje statue to the church and placed it near the front of the nave. It began to weep heavily in full view of the many people who were coming back to their pews from Communion. After a few moments of prayer, Carol noticed an overwhelming fragrance of roses, "like I was in the midst of a rose garden," she noted. "The person next to me grabbed my hand and was crying. Many people were overcome with emotion. There were no flowers in the church at all during this time because it was Lent."

Carol laughed in recalling this incident, remembering that later she had gone downstairs (the parish offices were in the basement of the church building) to see if she could find a source for the rose smell. She was also struck by the fact that not everyone could smell what she described as "like laying down in a rose garden."

APRIL 11, 1992

While hearing confessions today, Fr. Bruse blessed the pearl white rosary of a woman who had just confessed her sins. While they watched, the rosary's beads changed to a medium blue.

Tom Saunders described a similar event. "I was standing right beside Fr. Jim [in the narthex, or vestibule, of the church] when [it] happened. A lady handed him a pure white rosary, the beads were pure white. He put it in his hands and [then] gave it back to her. Every one of those beads was dark blue! I don't know who was more surprised, the lady or Fr. Jim."

APRIL 12, 1992
Palm Sunday

Tommy Schoegler was an altar boy at the 7:00 a.m. Mass this morning. Father Bruse was the celebrant. The Our Lady of Smiles statue wept so profusely that water puddled on its pedestal and on the floor. Father Bruse's wrists began to bleed as well, staining the sleeves of his alb, and Tommy reported that he seemed to be in great pain.

APRIL 16, 1992

Father Bruse and Fr. Hamilton joined most of the other Diocese of Arlington priests today in the celebration of the annual Chrism Mass at the Cathedral of St. Thomas. There was some speculation that the large statue of the Virgin Mary in the church might weep, but it did not. Reportedly, a smaller statue of Our Lady in the basement of the church wept after the services when Fr. Bruse went downstairs to meet with some visitors who desired a blessing.

His stigmata wounds bled substantially, running through his protective wrist bands and dripping onto his alb. Later that evening, Libby Lawler reported that she could see his wrists bleeding toward the end of the Holy Thursday service.

With the beginning of the Triduum, the statues of the Holy Family (including Our Lady of Smiles holding the Infant Jesus) were placed out of sight in the confessional room, awaiting Easter Sunday. Deacon Emil Myskowski reported that the statue was quietly weeping when he went to check on it.

APRIL 29, 1992

I met with Fr. Bruse today for an update on the "happenings." I was particularly interested in finding out if anything had occurred during the Easter Triduum, since many of us had anticipated that the stigmata wounds might be unusually active during this time, perhaps accompanied by visions of Christ's passion as other stigmatics had experienced. He told me that he had pain and heavy bleeding the night of Holy Thursday. He also experienced substantial pain in his stigmata wounds on Good Friday.

Father Bruse is hearing reports from several people that Madonna statues which he has blessed are weeping after they return to their homes. Often there is no crying by the statues at the time of the blessing.

On April 26, the Madonna with Infant statue in the church began weeping at the beginning of the 12:30 p.m. Mass and continued until at least 3:30 p.m. Tear flow was steady and heavy, running onto the floor before numerous witnesses.

During the interview, I asked Fr. Bruse to bless four Madonna statues belonging to friends. After he had done so, they all began to weep. One was a shiny white porcelain bust with crossed arms. The surface of this statue was so smooth that the tears would not adhere to the surface at all. The water collected in a small basin formed just inside the statue's left arm, as I discovered when I said to Fr. Bruse that I did not think that particular statue had wept. He simply turned the statue upside down and the water splashed onto his desk.

Father Bruse had a beautiful Our Lady of Grace statue atop a bookcase near his desk. This statue is identical to the one which he gave his mother and which initiated all the statuary weeping last November. The little statue wept profusely. (See Figure 1).

Unnoticed at the time was an apparent color change in one of the statues which I had brought to Fr. Bruse for blessing. It was a small (about 7 inches) Our Lady of Grace statue with a blue mantle and white robe with yellow highlights. When I returned the statue to my friend, he told me that the robe had been all white when he gave it to me. The coloring change is very similar to that which occurred in another Our Lady of Grace statue belonging to Isobel Milligan (see report of February 26, 1992).

Later that evening, Father Bruse met with Sister Mary Evelyn and some of her visiting family members. During his time with them, eight statues of the Blessed Virgin Mary wept.

MAY 2, 1992

Carol Marino brought her neighbor and her neighbor's child, David, to SEAS to make his first confession to Fr. Bruse. The boy took a small plastic statue of the Blessed Virgin Mary from his bedroom bookshelf and brought it along. It was very small and fit in his pocket. Fr. Bruse blessed both the boy and his statue and when the child emerged from the confessional, his statue was weeping "tiny little tears." Several of the persons present were moved to tears themselves just watching the child's innocent reverence as he watched his own statue weep.

MAY 8, 1992

Jacqueline Gordon noticed a pronounced fragrance of roses after Mass this morning. She, Carol Marino, and a few others had remained behind to discuss the things that had been going on. Carol also smelled the fragrance, as did some of the others, although not everyone experienced it with the same intensity. There were no flowers in the church. Fr. Bruse had already left for the rectory.

Elizabeth Spoth went to the rectory in mid-morning to meet with Marie Pelletier regarding some upcoming Parish Council business. Inside, she seated herself on a sofa while Marie was on the phone confirming an appointment for Fr. Bruse, who was waiting with his jacket on for the clearance to leave. Fr. Bruse had picked up a framed 8x10 photo of an Our Lady of Grace statue which is in Tihaljina,[2] not far from Medjugorje, and was kind of idly swinging it around the way people will do when their minds are preoccupied with something else. After Marie confirmed his appointment, he put the picture down and left. Pam Hood, who assisted in the rectory on Fridays, noticed something on the picture and got up to look at it. "Marie, look at this," she said. Then Elizabeth got up, also, to see what had happened to the picture. On it were several dime-sized droplets of water, directly down from the eyes, holding their position and shape against the tug of gravity. Marie took a tissue and dabbed the water from the glass covering the

---

[2]This portrait of the Blessed Virgin Mary statue at Tihaljina has become world famous because it is associated with the apparitions at Medjugorje. It is frequently found as the picture on prayer cards. The face is particularly lifelike and beautiful. The same Italian manufacturer which made this statue also made the lifesize Our Lady of Grace statue in the new church for Saint Elizabeth Ann Seton parish. This statue was not obtained by SEAS until the weeping phenomenon had ended.

photo, saying as she did so, "I was going to have Fr. Jim bless this, but... oh, well... "

MAY 10, 1992

Father Bruse spoke to a gathering of high school religious education students and teachers in the church basement this evening. There were some other parishioners present as well. Some brought religious objects to be blessed. A longtime friend of Pinkey's in Houston, Texas, sent up a whole box of objects to be blessed. These were all spread out on a table near the podium where Fr. Bruse spoke. He gave them a general blessing. None wept.

The next day, however, a lovely Fatima statue belonging to Pinkey's friend and present the evening before, was sitting on a buffet in our living room. Pinkey passed by in the course of the afternoon and noticed water flowing out of the statue's eyes and down its cheeks.

MAY 11, 1992

Father Bruse said the 9:00 o'clock morning Mass. Carol Marino noticed that he was favoring his wrists. As she approached for Communion, she saw that his stigmata wounds were bleeding and that he had blood spots on the inner wrist portion of his alb.

MAY 13, 1992

Members of the New Church Building Committee visited the Church of the Precious Blood in Culpeper, Virginia today. They are in the process of comparing architectural styles, color schemes, inside furnishings, etc., and just plain old looking for good ideas to incorporate into SEAS' new church building. John Garing, Marie Pelletier, Mary Mahler, Warren Walker and Fr. Bruse made the trip. As they walked around the inside of the church, they couldn't help noticing the images of the Blessed Virgin Mary and wondering whether any would weep. This day it was not Mary but her son, Jesus, who wept. When Fr. Bruse, who had tarried in the parking lot briefly, entered the church, a small (12-14") crucifix hanging on the wall began to cry. Tears ran down the stricken face of the crucified figure, dripped from the impaled feet, and puddled on the floor below. This was Mary Mahler's first experience with a statue weeping and she could hardly find words to express her astonishment.

MAY 22, 1992

Several persons at St. Elizabeth Seton Church on this Friday afternoon reported seeing rotating colors in clouds overhead. This was viewed by numerous people at different locations in Lake Ridge. Father Bruse described the sun as spinning rapidly and throwing off colors. Nearby clouds had bands of bright colors rippling through them with the color arrangement within the bands constantly changing.

On the same afternoon, about 2:00 p.m., Maura Gregory, her brother Jason, and his girlfriend, Amy, observed a similar strange display of colors in the sky. They were driving home down I-395 when they saw a bright, white, fluffy cloud with a band of colors through the middle of it. The cloud appeared to be resting over the highway.

Jason was the first to see it. "Gosh, that cloud up there is really pretty!" he said.

Maura described it later: "It wasn't like a rainbow. It was like a ribbon effect—you know, rippled, and it was as if it were just resting on the cloud. The colors were normal ones but they were so vivid! It was as though someone took a marker and just wrote on the cloud." After a few minutes, they simply drove under the cloud and it was left behind them.

MAY 23, 1992

This evening, after the 6:00 p.m. vigil Mass was over, the Our Lady of Smiles statue began to weep profusely. A woman who had remained behind to pray came outside, shaking, to tell Carol Marino and perhaps a dozen other people, including several from out of town, who had lingered in conversation near the entrance of the church. These few were deeply moved by crying which Carol described in her personal journal as "tears all on the cheeks, down the front of the dress; dress was soaked." The tearing went on for about half an hour.

Jacqueline Gordon took a photo of the statue weeping. When she had it developed, there was a discernible outline of a woman's veil in front of the statue, as if Jackie had taken the photo over the shoulder of a ghostly apparition.

Carol also noticed that during the Mass Fr. Bruse seemed to be having severe pain in his right hand area. His stigmata wounds were bleeding and hurting him greatly. Afterwards, he admitted he had been in too much pain to conceal it.

MAY 27, 1992

A friend of mine, Ty Cullen, told me about a spiritual healing involving use of some statue tear water which Pinkey had mixed with holy water and given to him. Ty gave it to a friend who lives in Gettysburg, Pennsylvania.

I spoke to Ty's friend, Mrs. Sandy Fitz. She is a nurse. Near the end of May, she was treating a patient in the hospital who was terminally ill with a massive infection of colon cancer metastasized to his liver. This 55-year old man was bitter and apparently heeding the advice of Dylan Thomas to not go gently into that "good night."

"You couldn't do anything to please him. He was in excruciating pain, really. You couldn't touch him," said Mrs. Fitz.

She and the man's wife took the tear/holy water and rubbed it all over his stomach. There was an immediate and wonderful reaction. "He just got such a peaceful look on his face—the pain was gone!" Mrs. Fitz reported. Although he died three days later, his whole attitude changed dramatically. He knew that something remarkable had happened to him. Instead of railing and cursing his fate, he became quiet and focused upon God. For two days, he even went off morphine. When he died on the third day, he told his wife, "I'm at peace. I'm going home."

MAY 30, 1992

On this Saturday, Pinkey received a call at home from Jon Jones, who was the teen worker at church that afternoon. He told her excitedly that a small Fatima statue was rotating its colors upstairs in the church. The statue belonged to a parishioner (reportedly Madelyn Webb) who had just gone to Fr. Bruse to confession. By the time Pinkey arrived, a crowd of 30-40 persons was gathered around watching the little foot-high statue change its colors.

Bob Capell, a parishioner, was also present that day, taking his turn at standing watch over the Madonna with Infant (Our Lady of Smiles) statue to ensure that it was not damaged by visitors who came to see the weeping statue they had heard about. The parishioner who owned the little Fatima statue began chatting with him and mentioned that Fr. Bruse had just blessed it. Bob asked to hold the statue because it seemed so pretty to him. A few moments later it began to change colors. "The base would be pink, then become yellow, then become blue. The cape would be blue, then yellow, then pink, then green," Bob reported. The phenomenon went on for about half an hour. The color changes were not flashes, like a neon light, but a slow replacement of one color with the next. There was no mistaking what was happening, however. "It was so visible, it was just incredible!" Bob would later say in describing it.

Two other parishioners who watched this, Amy and Tom Shaffer, described the color changing as "real slow" but unquestionable.

This phenomenon is reported to have happened twice more on successive Saturdays and several times previously with other statues. Another instance is described under the entry for September 11, 1992.

SPRING 1992

This is a story that was related to me by Libby Lawler in 1998. It had been earlier captured by Linda Christie in her report, but in both tellings the actual date was forgotten. It was during the time when the statues were still weeping, however.

Libby's mother, Mrs. Kitty Brennan, was 85 years old, legally blind, and suffered from a variety of ailments, including multiple shoulder dislocations to the point where she could no longer raise her arms above her head. Despite these sufferings, however, she was an extremely devout woman with a lifelong devotion to the Blessed Virgin Mary. For years, she had prayed the rosary daily and prayed constantly for her eight children. Libby's sister brought her to Lake Ridge for Fr. Bruse's blessing.

That night, Mrs. Brennan stayed at her daughter Libby's home, sleeping in a bedroom graced with several statues of the Blessed Virgin Mary. Sometime during the night, she heard a woman crying. She got up to investigate, but found no one in her room or the adjoining bathroom. The next morning, Libby offered the possibility that since her mother was too visually impaired to see the statues cry, that perhaps God was letting her share the experience this way. She then decided to stay in the room with her mother the following night, "in case anything should happen."

Sometime during the night, Libby awakened to hear "a woman's voice, a beautiful voice, saying, 'I love you, I love you.' Oh, it was just so beautiful!" In her groggy state, Libby simply assumed it was her mother speaking and responded, "I love you, too, Mom," and fell back asleep.

The next morning, Libby mentioned it to her mother, who said she had no recollection of speaking during the night. When her son, Michael, inquired about the sound of the voice, Libby realized that it had sounded nothing like her mother's voice, which was "extremely raspy" from a collapsed vocal chord.

EARLY JUNE 1992

One afternoon in early June, Dolores Rader, Gloria O'Brien and Denise Liss met at the church to pray and to view the Madonna with Infant statue, which was no longer being guarded constantly. There were only three other women in the church, and they left soon after Dolores and her two friends arrived.

"The statue itself was not weeping when we were there, but the whole base was just loaded with water—the entire base was saturated!" remembers Dolores. Denise had purchased a handkerchief earlier that day from People's Drugstore. It was sealed in plastic, which she tore off. She soaked the handkerchief in the collected tear water and then tore the cloth into three parts: keeping half for herself and giving one fourth to each of the other two women. When Dolores got home, she cut off a small strip for her brother in Pennsylvania and sealed the rest of the cloth in a plastic baggie to prevent evaporation. A day later, she decided to leave the bag open because there was mist inside it and she feared mildew. She did not handle the cloth.

A few days later, on the Feast of the Stigmatines (June 12), Dolores was talking about her piece of cloth to her neighbor and decided to retrieve it from her jewelry box where she had placed it. Still inside the plastic bag, inside the jewelry box, the small piece of cloth now had several bright red stains on it, bearing a striking resemblance to fresh blood stains. Calls to Gloria O'Brien and Denise Liss revealed that their pieces of the cloth were still white and unmarked.

Dolores also claimed to see the face of Christ in one of the red stains. When I saw the cloth for this report, nearly a year later, the stains had faded to a pink color and the face image, no more than 1/2 inch across, was difficult to ascertain. However, the shape of a head and two eyes is discernible; even a rough representation of a crown of thorns.

Dolores told me of another strange experience she had the afternoon she was standing before the statue with her two friends. She suddenly felt a drop of something strike her left hand and said jokingly to Gloria, "Your roof isn't leaking, is it?" A quarter-sized round patch of a viscous material was lying on the back of her hand. It did not move as she examined it, but when she touched it, it felt like chrism oil. She rubbed it into her hand. There was no one near the three women at this time; in fact, they were the only ones in the church. She is unable to identify any logical source for this oil.

During our interview, Dolores told me of visiting Our Lady of Angels Church one evening after Fr. Bruse had been there. The wooden Blessed Virgin statue in the vestibule had wept previously, but she was not sure exactly when in conjunction with this evening visit. She paused before the statue, said a few Hail

Marys, and noted that the eyes of the statue were in their usual half-closed position. After the meeting ended, she passed by the statue again. The eyes were not the same. "I swear those eyes were completely closed!" she says. By itself, one would suspect just a trick of lighting, but her experience is remarkably similar to that reported by Marcia Grattan, Linda Christie and the Aquinas students on March 17, 1992.

JUNE-JULY 1992

Father Bruse and his sister left on vacation in mid-June. While in South Dakota, they experienced a "miracle of the sun." On their way to a Passion Play one afternoon, they looked out the window of the bus they were riding in. The sun seemed to have a kind of protective filter over it so it was not difficult to view. Around the sun was a perfectly-formed golden ring. The sky between the sun and this huge gold ring was colored purple. Oddly, not everyone on the bus could see the phenomenon while it was occurring, although many could.

After their return in July, the Madonna with Infant statue in the church wept once or twice. These were the last reported weepings of this statue.

One afternoon, Marcia Grattan and some friends were talking outside the front entrance to SEAS church. All of them noticed a very pronounced odor of roses which came and went. There was no apparent natural explanation for this fragrance.

JULY 1992

People still congregate in front of the Madonna with Infant statue in church, some to pray, most probably hoping to see it weep. While this was taking place one day, Marcia Grattan and some friends noticed a couple of people in the sacristy of the church watching a small Fatima statue which was resting on a lace cloth. They drew closer and found the little statue was "just weeping and weeping."

JULY 6, 1992

A small Madonna statue wept in the sacristy after Mass this morning. Father Bruse had already left. About fifteen people witnessed the weeping and nearly everyone present also noticed a sweet scent of roses that permeated the room.

JULY 7, 1992

Madelyn Webb had a small statue that she was giving to a cancer patient. She placed it on a small table at the back of the church. After Mass, she went to retrieve it to give to Fr. Bruse for his blessing. Before she picked it up and before Fr. Bruse received it, it was already weeping so much that it stood in a small puddle of water. Fr. Bruse seemed as much in awe of the tears as anyone present.

JULY 26, 1992

Linda and Jack Christie visited a friend whose daughter attends Aquinas School. They had a Fatima statue which was a gift from Fr. Bruse. Reportedly, the statue was not only crying and changing its colors, but had become animated, as well. In Linda's own words:

> "I held the statue for many minutes as the [friends they were visiting] shared more stories with us. I kept looking at her face. She had a small smile with very lifelike eyes, but nothing seemed to change as I watched. Finally, I put it down and then just before we left, I picked it up again. The expression was definitely different and she was smiling more widely. I wouldn't be so sure of what I had seen except that then her mouth became drawn up, pursed. It was INCREDIBLE!!! [My friends] said, 'Yes, that's the way she's looked before, smiling. Now, Mrs. Christie, you'll be able to testify, too.'"

During subsequent visits to this family over the next ten days or so, Linda saw a two-foot plaster Fatima statue which Fr. Bruse had given to the family. On the first occasion, the statue's robe was a pale blue. At her next visit, the robe had become a vivid green.

AUGUST 15, 1992
Feast of the Assumption of Mary

Father Bruse celebrated the 9:00 a.m. Mass for the Feast of the Assumption of the Blessed Virgin Mary into heaven. Afterward, he and several other persons reported a strong scent of roses in the back of the church. The scent persisted even outside.

AUGUST 22, 1992

Father Bruse's stigmata wounds bled for the last time (reported anyway) today.

Media interest in the phenomena, starved by the lack of cooperation imposed by the edict from the Chancery, has waned. With it has gone most public attention. Only a few visitors and pilgrims continue to visit the church and seek out Fr. Bruse. Life at SEAS has returned almost to normal.

SEPTEMBER 1992

In early September, a group representing the *Jesus, King of All Nations Society*, brought a large oil painting of Jesus standing atop the world to SEAS to be blessed by Fr. Bruse. The figure of Jesus had an exposed Sacred Heart. The SEAS stop was an early point of their planned pilgrimage with the painting to Lourdes, Fatima and Russia. Pinkey happened to be in the back of the church that day. She saw Fr. Bruse bless the painting, which was up near the altar in front of the Madonna with Infant statue, by placing his hand over the heart of Jesus. When he removed his hand, a clearly discernible white cross lay on the heart.

Because of the distance from Pinkey to the painting and the fact that the heart has a white highlighting spot on it anyway, I was dubious of this particular report. However, in a subsequent interview in January 1998, Father Bruse confirmed that a white cross did appear on the heart at the time of his blessing. He, of course, was right in front of the painting and in position to judge any changes in shape or color.

SEPTEMBER 11, 1992

Father Bruse was visiting with Carol Marino and some others at Madelyn Webb's home. While there, they prayed the rosary and Carol brought a small Fatima statue for him to bless. After his blessing, he continued to hold it while the statue started changing colors. Carol was particularly struck by a deep, vibrant orange which spread through parts of the statue which previously had been white. Some 25 persons were present.

NOVEMBER 21, 1992

Today, Father Bruse addressed a meeting of the Magnificat Society, a Marian devotional group, at the Hilton Hotel in Springfield, Virginia. There were some small Madonna statues present. After Fr. Bruse's departure, an Our Lady of Grace statue began to weep and a Fatima statue changed its colors.

Elizabeth Poel was one of the attendees at this conference. She told me that she came to St. Elizabeth Ann Seton Church later that afternoon to go to confession to Father Bruse. She had been suffering from chronic pain in her right shoulder and hand, which her physician had said could not be cured because it was just "part of aging." After Fr. Bruse's blessing, however, her pain disappeared and nearly four years later had not returned.

THANKSGIVING 1992

Just before the Thanksgiving holiday began, Libby Lawler took a framed picture of Our Lady of Medjugorje (Figure 11) with her to the 11:00 a.m. daily children's Mass at Our Lady of Angels Church. She intended to have Fr. Bruse, who celebrated the Mass that morning, bless it for her mother whom she was about to visit at her home in Pennsylvania. After the Mass was over, she found Fr. Bruse and Marie Pelletier outside, looking at the sky. Libby asked, "What are you looking at?"

Marie responded, "The sun is spinning. Look at the sun."

"I looked at the sun, without any hesitation at all," Libby told me. "I started to cry immediately because I could actually see it spinning. It was going very rapidly and there was also other movement. I didn't see any colors or anything like that." Later, Libby described this other movement as "pulsating, in and out, very rapidly."

Shortly afterward, Sister Mary Evelyn came out of the church and asked, "What's going on?"

Libby replied, "The sun is spinning."

But when Sister Mary Evelyn looked up, she could not see what the others were seeing. In fact, she saw only the glare of the harsh, noontime sun, which promptly gave her spots before her eyes—a warning of possible damage to the retina.

A few weeks later, when Fr. Bruse came to Our Lady of Angels for another daily Mass, Libby tried looking at the sun again. Nothing but spots before her eyes this time. After this experience, she vowed to be less hungry for miracles, noting that such phenomena can be so exciting that one just wants more and more.

A few months later, following a Saturday evening Mass at SEAS, Libby and her son, Michael, were in the parking lot when suddenly she "just had a feeling that something was going to happen." Because of her promise to stop looking for miraculous signs, she was hesitant to look up. So she asked Michael to see if the sun was spinning.

He looked and said, "Yeah, it is."

FEBRUARY 3, 1993

Pinkey visited Fr. Bruse in his office at the rectory around noon today. After chatting a bit, Fr. Bruse left the office briefly, leaving Pinkey admiring the little Our Lady of Grace statue which he keeps on top of his bookcase (see Figure 1). She said a silent prayer and was startled to see the small statue's eyes well up with tears which then rolled down its cheeks. She also noticed what appeared to be a light chrism oil around the base of the statue. Later we learned that apparently some statues are exuding oil now. The tears she saw may have been oil, as well, since she did not touch them or attempt to ascertain their composition.

JUNE 14-15, 1993

Pinkey has been admitting pilgrims into the church during the late afternoon period when it is locked after the staff has gone home. On these two days, when she has locked up prior to her own departure, she noticed a very strong odor of roses while standing at the back of the nave in the church. There were no flowers around to account for the scent. In fact, the flowers before the Our Lady of Smiles statue at the front of the nave were wilted and dying.

Later, Johanna Gregory told her of similar aromatic experiences that other persons were reporting.

HEALINGS

Perhaps no demonstration of the presence of the divine has more impact than a miraculous healing. They cause dramatic changes in the lives of those affected and excite the hopes of others who are suffering physical pains, anxieties and hardships that the rest of us who are healthy can only pity and dread. Such events are never characterized as "trivial" or unimportant. Nothing else conveys the compassion and presence of God so powerfully. Have there been miraculous healings at SEAS?

At various times, I have heard reports of numerous miraculous cures. An old man apparently suffering from terminal cancer in January or February 1992 was blessed by Fr. Bruse and then, reportedly, appeared in church a couple of weeks later completely healthy.

Linda Christie passed on a story she heard from a friend about a man who fell and hurt himself badly enough to need spinal surgery. Although the surgery was risky, doctors told him he would die without it. Then Fr. Bruse blessed him and his pain went away. Reportedly, two separate examinations with x-rays have indicated that surgery for this man is no longer required.

Confirmation of these reports has often been difficult to come by, however. Since there was no organized effort to offer healing services, nor, for that matter, did Fr. Bruse perceive that he had received this particular gift, accurate names, dates and places were usually not written down anywhere. As a general rule, documentation was not pursued.

In some cases, the beneficiaries of cures have been reluctant to share the news of their great blessing for fear of excessive public attention. This is the situation with what is probably the best known and well documented miraculous healing here, the case referred to in the *U.S. News and World Report* cover story on Fr. Bruse, "The Case of the Weeping Madonna," (March 29, 1993). That was the young girl reportedly cured of blindness and cancer.

Other healings which were reported to me include the following:

PHYLLIS. Phyllis was a middle-aged woman who suffered from emphysema and severe lung disease. Her condition was life-threatening and she was a candidate for lung replacement.

In the winter of 1994, Phyllis was back in the hospital, suffering from pneumonia. She was on a respirator in the intensive care unit and doing poorly. Her friend, Corene Teneriello, visited her that day and was shocked by her appearance. "I just didn't think she was going to be alive the next morning. She looked gray," reported Corene. Phyllis lay unconscious throughout the visit. Corene went home fearing the worst for her dear friend.

On the drive home, Corene remembered a remarkable story she had heard from members of her family about statues weeping at a Catholic church in Lake Ridge, Virginia. Her nephew, Tom Croce, a parishioner of SEAS, had collected some of the tear water from one of the crying episodes by the Our Lady of Smiles statue and sent it to his mother. She, in turn, parceled it out to members of the family, including her sister-in-law, Corene. Thinking that maybe the tear water, miraculously produced, might also have special blessings from its use, Corene grabbed her small bottle and her husband and returned to the hospital that evening.

Corene, a no-nonsense lady of deep faith but skeptical of anything resembling magical potions and the like, asked her husband to stand watch at the door while she applied some of the tear water to her friend. Using the water, she made the sign of the cross on Phyllis' forehead and prayed, "Dear God, please let her make it through the night." The time was around 9:00 or 10:00 p.m.

The next day, Corene called the hospital, fearing the worst. She was astonished to learn that Phyllis had made a dramatic recovery. She was removed from the respirator and went home from the hospital a few days later.

Later Corene told Phyllis about the incident and gave her the remainder of the small bottle of tear water, suggesting she bless herself with it whenever she had a bad night. Ultimately, Phyllis received her lung transplant and today is living fairly normally.

Although Phyllis' daughter later noted that her mother had had previous bouts when she appeared to be slipping away, and had recovered, Corene had never seen her look so desperately sick as on that cold night in 1994. She is convinced that the blessing with the tear water saved her friend's life and was instrumental in maintaining her stability until the transplant could take place.

FRANK. Frank was a diabetic with severe heart trouble who attended Mass at SEAS in late March 1992. Fr. Bruse was the celebrant. During the Mass Frank felt some pain in his chest but decided to stick it out. Thereafter, he felt his pain decrease to a point he hadn't felt in years. He went to a local fire station and asked the rescue crew to perform an EKG on him. The results indicated his heart was stronger than it had been. Frank's diabetes also affected his feet, so much so that he could wear only athletic shoes. In the week following his attendance at the Mass, however, his feet improved to the point where he was able to wear regular shoes again.

CHRISTOPHER. A cure which in mystery rivals that of the girl mentioned in the *U.S. News and World Report* story concerns the grandson of Fran Perotti's cousin. Fran's relatives in New Jersey had heard about the strange goings on down here. Christopher, the six-year old grandson of his cousin, was very ill with what the doctors characterized as "idiopathic pancreatitis with multiple pseudo cysts," or severe inflammation of the pancreas of unknown causes. The child was listless, unable to eat or drink easily, and seemingly headed downhill with a hole in his pancreas. At his grandmother's urging, his parents brought him to SEAS over the Memorial Day weekend in 1992.

On Sunday, May 24, Christopher visited at Bob Perotti's home in Manassas. While there, Mrs. Perotti had him bless himself with some statue tear water which she had obtained from Fr. Bruse's mother and which she kept in a vial. Christopher dipped his hand into the water and made the sign of the cross on himself. Immediately, he said, "Boy, my hand is hot! It feels real hot!"

The next morning, Christopher and his parents gathered for daily Mass at SEAS. Before the Mass, Fr. Bruse blessed the boy. That afternoon, Christopher was eating and drinking with all the gusto of any normal six-year old boy.

When they returned to New Jersey, Christopher's parents took him back to his doctor, who was astonished to see such activity and robustness in the previously gravely-ill child. X-rays and ultrasound scans revealed an inexplicable "film" covering the hole in his pancreas. His mother told Fran, "Whatever that priest did, [Christopher] has been running around and playing ever since the day he came home! He goes to school, he drinks his milk, which he couldn't drink..." Christopher's medical follow-ups have become less and less frequent as he continues to show no symptoms of illness.

HEATHER. Another reported case of healing concerns a young woman named Heather. She was a nineteen year old girl diagnosed as having breast cancer. Amy Shaffer provided her with a piece of lace which had been soaked in statue tear water. At a healing service which Heather attended, the lace was placed on her chest. The next day, when she went into the hospital for surgery, the doctors discovered no trace of cancer. Heather has no hesitation in attributing her cure to a miraculous intervention.

DENISE. Maura Gregory had a young friend who was diagnosed with a breast lump in December 1992. The night before her surgery, Maura gave Denise her rosary to take with her to the hospital. This is the same rosary which had inexplicably changed in color from silver to gold the previous January (see Rosary Color Changes, below). The next day, there was no breast lump to be found.

BARBARA ADAMS. This remarkable case involves a family who moved to Lake Ridge from Alabama in March 1993. Barbara Adams and her family attended Mass at SEAS for the first time on March 27. The next morning, she and her husband were cleaning up and making breakfast when she inadvertently picked up a cup which she had just filled with grease from frying bacon. The cup was so hot that she lost control of it and spilled the hot grease all over the fingers of her right hand. She was horrified. Just a month before she had scalded the same hand in hot tap water and ended up with it badly swollen and needing constant soaking in a burn lotion.

Realizing the grease burn would be far more severe than the water scalding, Barbara's husband, Tony, said: "Let's just go to the hospital!" Barbara hesitated, her hand under running water from the sink faucet, thinking she should remove the grease first. "All of a sudden I realized I had no pain whatsoever," she remembers. "I pulled [my hand] out from under the spigot and I looked at it and it was absolutely radiant, almost like new skin! It was... peachy... beautiful... smooth... it was radiant!" she said. "At that moment, it was as if I were in the church, looking at the statue [Our Lady of Smiles] of Mary and Jesus. And I clearly heard the words, 'This is the first of many [miracles] to happen now that you are here.'" Barbara says, "It was like I was transported there for a moment. Everything was tuned out around me for those brief moments." She believes strongly that the beautiful male voice which she heard "was the voice of Jesus."

CHRIS VOGEDING. Not all persons who were blessed by Fr. Bruse or who treated their illnesses with the statue tear water have been blessed with physical cures. It is safe to say that most were not healed. But the blessings and the grace which came with them were always bountiful.

In January 1993, Pinkey and I sent a small bottle of tear water mixed with holy water to a dear friend in California who was suffering from terminal breast cancer. Although she reported some physical improvement in her condition, she was, sadly, not cured. She is not unique. Other persons have failed to improve and have died. This mystery of God's will shall not be sorted out by us here on earth. We are left to remember that the world we cannot see is vastly more beautiful and joyous than the one in which we live. Our sorrow in faith, therefore, can only be for ourselves, left behind. It is hard for us to accept, but there is a greater miracle involved than the mere physical healing. Our friend, Chris Vogeding, expressed this very well in her letter to us responding to the tear water which we sent her:

> "It is not that I am expecting a miracle from the tears, but there has been one of my spirit. I don't think I ever doubted God's existence and, heaven knows, I call on Him numerous times day and night. Still, it is so moving, touching, so very life altering to know God is physically showing us that He is real. And on days when our faith flounders, we can reflect on how much He loves each and every one of us. This knowledge gives me great joy when I think of the family I'll be leaving behind. They are going to have a horrible time adjusting to my death but if they can just hold on to the feeling that the Lord is there for them, maybe the transition won't be so hard."

These eloquent words from Chris reveal a much more important healing: the transformation of weak faith into the certainty that God exists and loves us. If the tears of the Queen of Peace wash away our doubts and fears without restoring earthly vitality, who could not say, "Thank you, Lord," even if the prayer must be whispered through our tears?

RACHEL PEVARNIK. Rachel entered God's kingdom on September 1, 1992, just one month short of her third birthday. She had received numerous blessings from Fr. Bruse, and even was nearly bathed in statue tear water. Yet God called her home after she had spent half her little life battling cancer. There is nothing quite so unsettling to our sense of good order and harmony in the universe than the premature death of children. Yet death is entirely the wrong concept because, as St. Francis of Assisi explained so eloquently, "in dying we are born to eternal life." Nonetheless, for the grieving parents, the loss of the child is a pain like no other and "death," indeed, seems not only the perfect description but perhaps even the perfect solution to their own sorrow and suffering.

The miracle in these cases is not the physical healing, but the gift of faith, of insight, of hope, of understanding that LIFE is on the *other* side of death's curtain; that a more accurate description of death is "doorway." Every person on earth will walk through that doorway sooner or later. In the meantime, the Blessed Mother of God's miracles of statues crying and other signs of her presence are a consolation to us all that we are surrounded by the supernatural.

Rachel's family knows that she is in heaven, a place of indescribable beauty and happiness. Her loss is a cross which they will carry all their lives. But her joy is theirs as well. Time will reunite them more quickly than any of us can imagine until we look back on our own lifetimes and discover that, no matter the number of their years, they vanished in the blink of an eye. In the meantime, Rachel's spirit remains vital and alive, not only in memory, but in reality as well.

Six months before she died, on the day her parents learned her remission from cancer had ended, Rachel walked up behind them as they knelt and prayed fervently before a crucifix. As a child will do, she patted each on the back. It may have been simply a gesture of affection, but surely those tiny hands were guided by the Holy Spirit because, today, Joe tells us, "he feels that pat on the back every day."

THE MIRACLE OF THE SUN

Anyone who is familiar with the reported apparitions of the Blessed Mother at the village of Medjugorje in Croatia, a province of Yugoslavia, will recognize stories of the phenomenon known as the "miracle of the sun." This experience involves the ability to gaze directly into the daytime sun and see it spinning, often throwing off a multitude of colors, perhaps pulsating, and not uncommonly accompanied by other patterns or silhouettes. The experience has not been a common one at St. Elizabeth Seton Church, but it has been reported (see entry for May 22 and Thanksgiving 1992, above). The following description by Jackie Tucker, however, may be one of the most vivid descriptions of this phenomenon which you will ever read.

September 4, 1992, was a sad day at St. Elizabeth Ann Seton Church. This was the day of two-year old Rachel Pevarnik's funeral. The pain of her loss lay crushingly upon her family and those who remembered the spirit and spunkiness of the beautiful little cancer victim. Although there is no doubt that Rachel was then laughing and playing with angels in the presence of our Blessed Mother, for those left behind the void of such a loss often seems impossible to fill.

After the funeral, Jackie Tucker returned to her home, unable to accompany the procession to the cemetery because of family obligations. Rachel's funeral brought home again all the terrible sorrow she had felt at the loss of her beloved older brother in April 1990. As she sat disconsolate in her living room, emotionally drained and saddened beyond words or tears, she felt an overwhelming desire to go outside. She walked out onto the deck overlooking her backyard. Her two children, Andy and Gracie, were playing inside.

"I just stood on the deck and I just kept sensing something. I could feel a real presence," she remembers. She stared idly at the trees in her backyard and let her eyes follow up through the foliage to the tops and into the sky where the sun was blazing in its midday brightness. That's when it happened. "In just a moment's time, I could literally see the rays leave the sun, entirely leave the sun. The sun itself became a ball and there was this protective cover which came over the sun so I could easily look at it without squinting. And then, instantly, the sun began spinning in a clockwise motion. I mean spinning very, very fast. Then the spinning would stop and it would pulsate. Then it would spin again. As this was starting to happen, the most incredible purple rained down on me. I couldn't leave the deck. I felt paralyzed. I kicked the door open and screamed for the kids. They came out and then it just escalated. It got more purple, it started spewing out all kinds of colors. It was like a laser show. As soon as they came out, we joined hands and fell to our knees because we really felt it was Christ and Mary."

Throughout this period, Jackie remembers her neighbor continued to mow his lawn, so obviously this incredible experience of hers and her children was not a meteorological phenomenon, but a subjective spiritual one.

The whole experience lasted 30-40 minutes. When it was over, she came inside and called the rectory, reaching Marie Pelletier. "I remember her saying to me," recalls Jackie, "that she went over to Fr. Jim and she started to tell him what I was obviously spitting out over the phone, and Jim said to Marie that he knew, that it was happening at the cemetery but he didn't feel that anyone else could see it."

About three weeks later, Jackie's parents came down from Syracuse for a family visit. Hesitantly, but earnestly, she prayed that they might share her experience of the "miracle of the sun."

In the afternoon after the parents arrived, Jackie and her mother were sitting on the back deck. Her father was napping. "I had a real sense of a smell—I could smell roses. But I didn't say anything to my mother." After awhile, Jackie and her mother went out to the front of the house.

There, her mother suddenly said to her, "When did you get a rose bush? Do you smell roses? Gosh, I smell roses!" The Tuckers have no rose bushes.

While her mother returned inside the house, Jackie walked up her steep hillside driveway to retrieve the evening newspaper. That's when the sun signs began again. She screamed for her mother, who rushed outside. "Look at it with your heart," advised Jackie. "Open your heart to this." Her mother looked up and she just started screaming. "Oh, my God!" she exclaimed, and started crying.

After a moment, Jackie's mother ran down the hill and roused her sleeping husband, whom Jackie describes as "a little Archie Bunker type—very skeptical."

But when he looked into the sky, his skepticism vanished. Later, her father would describe his vision of the sun phenomenon in much the same terms as Jackie but he saw what appeared to be brown sticks emerging without any apparent pattern or order from the golden, disk-like sun.

Courtney Tucker, Jackie's husband, was in Orlando, Florida on September 4, 1992, when the first sun experience occurred. He was home for subsequent experiences but has never seen what the other family members describe. Still, he is not a skeptic. He does not suspect a kind of communal hysteria, a suspicion which has probably already occurred to many who are reading these lines. Why not, I wondered.

Courtney explains: "I have looked at Jackie's face and I've seen other people looking at the sun, literally with their eyes wide open, no tearing, no squinting, just like I'm looking at you now. I would look the same way that they were looking and I would have to squint and tears would be streaming down because you can't look at the sun!"

Jackie subsequently had her eyes examined by an ophthalmologist without disclosing the extraordinary activity to which she had been exposing them. He reported that her eyes were fine; in fact, had improved a little.

A final bit of corroborative evidence: when six-year old Gracie was asked to draw what she had seen, she drew a large, round, multi-colored sun, using lines to indicate a clockwise spinning motion.

Jackie's deceased brother, Paul, was born October 25, 1951. In October 1992, Jackie went home to New York to participate in an anniversary Mass and visit to Paul's gravesite. Jackie remembers that day in Syracuse as cold and intermittently snowy under a thick cloud cover. Her brother had died in her arms, precisely as the "amen" was pronounced at the end of the Our Father on April 8, 1990. Now the family members held hands around his gravestone and, once again, recited the Lord's Prayer.

Jackie remembers: "Precisely at 'amen,' the sun came out, spun wildly and shot off colors all over us. One niece started to run. I started to cry. My sister, I remember her so well screaming and holding her face, saying 'Oh, my God!' She started to cry. I just said to them: 'Come back! You give thanks; you give thanks right now!'" They said the Hail Mary and, "as quickly as it came, it went." About ten family members were in attendance and viewed this phenomenon.

Later that afternoon, sensing that her youngest brother, Patrick, was deeply troubled by his experience at Paul's gravesite, Jackie went on a walk with him in the rural countryside to a place where Paul used to like to play and picnic with the children. The gray, deeply-overcast sky lay heavily upon the landscape, lightened only occasionally by a brief flurry of snow. Patrick seemed on the verge of tears. Jackie then had that strange sensation which by now she had come to recognize as the harbinger of awesome signs in the sky. She warned Patrick that "something's going to happen here." What followed was a strange sensation that Jackie calls a "rumbling with no sound." Immediately, a triangular shape opened in the dense cloud cover, revealing a beautiful pink color in the sky as a gorgeous sun emerged. Within the triangle, the sun began to spin, casting off brilliant hues in every color of the rainbow.

"Patrick just said, 'Is this real?'

"And I pinched him and said, 'Yeah, it's here and it's happening!'" In a few moments, the phenomenon was gone and the gray clouds once again hung low and still.

This "miracle of the sun" experience is one which Jackie and her family members now experience regularly, including the day this interview was conducted (June 16, 1993). As Jackie tells it: "I have been in situations, like on a soccer field or something, where I won't even say anything to him [Andy], and he'll stop and then we'll compare later."

Courtney corroborated this and added: "Jackie would get on the phone and call the family in Syracuse. They're both seeing the same thing at the same time, four hundred miles apart!"

What has all this meant to Jackie's family? It has had a tremendous impact on their spirituality. Her father is no longer an "Archie Bunker skeptic." Her sister, who had fallen away from her faith, now goes to Mass "all the time."

"The experience has totally touched my family like you wouldn't believe!" declares Jackie.

In April 1993, Jackie and her sister, Kathleen, experienced the "miracle of the sun" while in the parking lot at SEAS on their way to attend an anniversary Mass for Paul. In this episode, Jackie saw the silhouette of a woman in a robe backlit by the veiled sun. Kathleen saw it, too, but more briefly. We can understand, therefore, the heartfelt conviction when Jackie says to us: "It is real. Truly in my heart I do believe it is the Blessed Mother. I really do."

While discussing some of this with John Garing, head of the parish building committee, one afternoon, I was surprised to hear him say that he, too, had seen the "miracle of the sun" three or four times. The first occasion was in February 1993 when Marie Pelletier called him at work and told him to look out his window. When he did so, he saw the sun covered by a disk, spinning rapidly in a counterclockwise direction, and throwing off a stunning profusion of vivid colors. Interestingly, he remembers the sun spinning in the opposite direction from the Tuckers' visions. John is a retired air force colonel.

Libby Lawler's experiences with this particular phenomenon are described on pp. 53-54. One of the interesting parallels between her experience and that of Jackie Tucker is that both had a strange sensation that something was about to happen before the sun miracle took place. One might liken this to a gentle nudge from God, saying: "I have something to show you." It may also serve as a practical reminder to the rest of us not to go staring at the sun until we, too, are "nudged" by God or, at least, invited by someone who says it is occurring at that moment.

Undoubtedly, there are many other members of this parish who have seen similar signs in the sun and sky but have not disclosed them outside their immediate family and friends. Father Bruse, for example, referred to "five or six very reliable" parishioners who told him in January 1993 about seeing the "miracle of the sun."

ROSARY COLOR CHANGES

There have been numerous rosary color changes reported at SEAS during the past year and a half (1991-93). Some of these are reported in the journal entries above. Most were associated directly with Fr. Bruse by a blessing or his personal handling of the rosary. But there are at least a couple of cases in which the rosary was never in Fr. Bruse's presence. To my mind, these occurrences simply reinforce the fact that Our Lady has been in our vicinity in a very real way the past 18 months or so.

FATHER BRUSE. There is no better source of rosary and other religious object color changes than Fr. Bruse. He has had many, many experiences of this. Some are rather amusing. As he tells it: "I've had people send me rosary beads to be blessed. And when I've sent them back, they've called up and said, 'You sent me the wrong ones.' They changed color!"

MAURA GREGORY. Maura Gregory, daughter of Ernie and Johanna Gregory, had an old silver rosary which she hung on a bedpost at the head of her bed. The rosary had been purchased years earlier in a hospital gift shop and was unremarkable in every way.

During the Christmas holiday in 1991, Maura's aunt and uncle visited the family in Lake Ridge. They stayed in Maura's bedroom and later commented on the silver rosary beads which Maura had hanging on her bedpost.

Some time after Maura returned to college in early January, 1992, her entire rosary changed from silver to gold in color. She has had the rosary examined by three jewelers, none of which could explain the color change. Following the advice of one, she attempted to clean the rosary of its possible "tarnishing." The gold color did not budge.

Both Maura and her mother say the rosary, beads and chain, feels "softer" now.

MARCIA GRATTAN. Marcia Grattan first found out about the weeping statues and Fr. Bruse's stigmata a week before the story broke on Channel 9 (March 6, 1992). Early television news reports included one lady who claimed her rosary changed color. As Marcia tells it, "I'm sitting there with Bill [her husband] and, even though I had seen the statue cry, we looked at each other and started to laugh. I said, 'They need to call up the guys with the white jackets and take that woman away!' little knowing that I'd be talking about myself!"

About a week later, on March 14, Marcia attended Saturday morning Mass at SEAS. After Mass was over, she watched, fascinated, as a long line of people waited patiently for Fr. Bruse to bless them or some religious object they were carrying. One of the people in line was a secretary whom Marcia knew from Aquinas School. The lady invited Marcia to join the line, which she did, then realized she hadn't brought anything for Fr. Bruse to bless. Suddenly, she remembered a rosary which she had recently purchased from a group accompanying the Pilgrim Virgin statue (Fatima) when it had come to Our Lady of Angels Church the month before. This inexpensive rosary was made of olive wood from Jerusalem. She presented it to Fr. Bruse. "I held it in my hand and he put his hand on top of it and blessed it."

After Marcia left the line, she began conversing with another couple who were standing there. "For some reason, I opened up my hand and I'm looking at these red splotches on my rosary. I picked it up to see if maybe I had a cut in my hand—no cut." She then checked inside her purse to see if a red felt-tipped pen might have leaked on the rosary, but there were no pens in that part of her purse and, anyway, they all were capped.

"I ran up to [a nun from Aquinas School]. I'm a little bit hysterical. I'm crying. I'm shaking. And I said, 'Look at this rosary. It's turning red!' She picked up the rosary and held it in such a way that no beads were touching one another and we continued to watch more beads turn red in front of our eyes!" This continued as other persons approached but ended when the rosary left the church.

JOHN GARING. While chatting outside Our Lady of Angels Church one Saturday, John showed me a little chaplet he had been carrying around since November 1992. A chaplet, at least in one form, is a single decade of the rosary joined at a center piece with a crucifix and the initial beads of a rosary. This one had chain links of a dark, brassy color. The chaplet was given to John not long after Fr. Bruse had blessed it. One day, a few months later, in March, John pulled it out of his pocket and discovered that his little chaplet had changed its coloring. The middle link in the three-link set dividing each bead had turned a bright silver. Where the chain was a little longer, two of the middle links were silver.

A PERSONAL EXPERIENCE. My own rosary changed the color of its chain. This occurred in January 1993. I remember thinking, as I read and heard of other persons having their rosaries change color, that I would enjoy that experience. However, since my own rosary had brown coco beads and the embossed figure of Mary was already turning a reddish color where the silver coating had been worn away, it did not seem a good candidate for a spontaneous, miraculous color change.

Then one day in mid-January, when I picked up the rosary to pray, I noticed something different about it. I realized all the chain had turned gold. The center piece with the image of Mary remained the same: coppery-looking where the finish had been worn off, and the crucifix was still silver-colored. A handful of chain links also still retained some traces of the silver finish.

Most of the people to whom I mentioned this reacted in a way which I did not expect. Polite but obviously skeptical. But I like skeptics. They keep us intellectually honest. My high school religious education students were more accepting. They wondered if the metal in the rosary had changed to real gold. This was a thought I had not considered. To begin with, the chain, although gold in color, did not look as yellow and shiny as the real gold chains which I had seen. Further, it seemed inherently improbable that a relatively inexpensive rosary would be converted by God into one much more materially valuable. He doesn't seem to operate that way very often. Nonetheless, I finally took the rosary to Kolb & Company, a jeweler in Woodbridge.

"The chain is brass," reported Ron Kolb, the jeweler. For a moment I was taken aback. Brass is normally yellow in color, so maybe there was no miraculous color change at all; perhaps I had simply forgotten what color the chain had been all along since this is the kind of thing we usually just don't notice. Yet I distinctly remembered thinking how nice it would be if my rosary changed to gold. I remembered noting that the Mary figure seemed to be changing slowly, albeit obviously from wear and tear from use and not from divine intervention. Further, the color was more red than gold, suggesting that the base metal, at least of the center piece, was copper. I decided to investigate further by trying to find a new rosary identical to my own.

W. Gallery, the religious goods store in Wheaton, Maryland, has a rosary in its 1993 catalog which is identical to mine. It is described as having brown oval coco beans and "silver-plated chain with double-wire construction." The crucifix and center piece depicted look exactly like my own. I ordered one with the thought that I could compare my present rosary with this one and maybe even have the new one's basic metal determined. Such a comparison would not be conclusive, of course, but it would be another piece of evidence. Unfortunately, the rosary which arrived was not the one pictured in the catalog and not identical to mine. When I returned it to W. Gallery, the clerk informed me that the manufacturers sometimes alter their designs and ship the new versions without bothering to disclose the changes.

I am convinced, however, that the chain did change its color overnight by suddenly and inexplicably losing its silver coating. A few of the beads still have tiny traces of silver on them, which would make no sense if the chain had not been entirely silver-coated at one time. Also, I have never seen a rosary with a gold color scheme which did not also have a matching color for the center piece and crucifix.

So, what's the point of all this explanation about a very minor miracle? First, it indicates the attitude I have tried to bring to this investigation. Skeptics and cynics love to dismiss people who accept the reality of miracles as being "credulous," meaning naive and foolish. In this report, I have laid out the facts as I witnessed them myself or as they were given to me. It is now incumbent upon the "Doubting Thomases" to examine these facts and explain how natural causes or trickery could have produced the results reported.

Second, it is a reminder that often God's "little" miracles have a note of ambiguity about them. I think that is His intention. As with all our beliefs in God and Christianity, there is always that little gap at the end which we cannot quite close with our reasoning and empirical data. That little gap requires the "leap of faith" to bring us to full acceptance of God and His here-and-now presence in our lives. This is the faith which Jesus valued so highly in the Roman Centurion who asked Jesus to heal his sick servant and which we commemorate for ourselves in the communion rite of every Mass. This faith is the price of admission into God's kingdom. Faith is the bridge between God and man and while we may not always understand why God is not more manifest in our physical world, we know from Scripture[3] and experience that without trust and faith there can be no personal relationship with God.

Third, and most important, all the little "signs and wonders" which we have had here have only one purpose: to draw our attention to the reality and presence of God and His Son, Jesus Christ. Once we have fully accepted this, God's grace will transform our lives. Scripture takes on new life and meaning. Mary and the saints become living friends always present to hear an entreaty and offer consolation. Prayer seems not so much to be hopeful thoughts and words cast into the void but more like a dialogue which is heard and answered in language other than speech. We should be grateful for the miracle of these signs which we have had here at SEAS. But they are not intended to be a substitute for faith and prayer. In fact, if they do not lead you to much greater faith and prayer, then they were, indeed, wasted on you.

There may be another reason, however, for my particular rosary change. At the time it occurred, I was debating whether to write this report at all. The diocese had made it clear since the previous March that it would not pay any attention to the phenomena surrounding Father Bruse. Both Father Bruse and Father Hamilton were concerned about this project somehow being in contravention of Bishop Keating's order to them to not promote the occurrences

---

[3]See, for example, Mk 6:5-6, where Jesus is so distressed by the lack of faith in his Nazareth acquaintances that he can hardly work any miracles, and Jn 20:29, where Jesus tells Thomas that those who believe without seeing are the ones who are blessed.

for the faithful, although as a lay member of the parish I was not bound by any such order. There were some suspicions that I was exploiting the unique access which I had enjoyed in gathering the information for this report. Pinkey was a staff member at St. Elizabeth Ann Seton parish and could expect to take a lot of heat if this report met with active opposition from her boss, the pastor. At this moment of critical indecision, I think God sent me this little miracle to give me the push I needed to go ahead with the report. Without it, there would be no formal record of the most extensive weeping statue, etc., display in the history of the Church, except for a few scattered secular newspaper and magazine reports. Surely, this would be cause enough to make Our Blessed Mother weep over our stony hearts and blasé attitudes.

BOTTOM LINE: miracles have little or no value unless they are known, shared and accepted as invitations by a kind and gracious God to come back to an active relationship with Him. They are simply attention-getters. Even miraculous healings are insignificant in their benefits for the body when compared to the eternal welfare of the soul. The real message for us is that God is real, Jesus Christ exists, the Blessed Virgin Mary is actively working in the world we live in, and our destiny is eternal. In a world of technological marvels and astonishing special effects, God has reminded us that He is here, that nothing has changed in His divine plan for the salvation of mankind. We must return to an active life of prayer, Scripture study, and participation in the sacraments. We must recapture our love for God and all things holy. We must live each day of our lives with the full understanding that we are pilgrims in this life, journeying toward an immortal destination which will be determined for each one of us by standards which have nothing to do with power, money and temporal success. When you do these things, you will then experience the greatest miracle of them all: the transformation of your soul.

AN INTERVIEW WITH FATHER JAMES BRUSE

[This interview took place in January and August 1998 with Father Bruse in the rectory of his parish, Saint Francis de Sales Catholic Church, Kilmarnock, Virginia.]

Q: Has there been a continuation of the "phenomena" here in Kilmarnock since you became pastor here in June 1995?

A: Not really, other than an occasional reported healing. We have had healing services here from time to time and some people may have been cured of illness. However, we have not tried to confirm these reports.

Although the large number of statues weeping and changing color and other things which happened at Saint Elizabeth Ann Seton Church have not followed me here, there have been rosaries which have changed color.

Q: What has been the effect on you of all that happened?

A: From what I have seen and what I experienced, I am able to say that, yes, there is a God who is close, who is not in a distant universe somewhere but a God who is with us. By seeing the conversions which happened I have seen how I can bring the Lord to people, to reach out to them. It's opened my faith up much more spiritually, wanting to help people to see that Christ is real. He's a God who is love—total Love!

What happened at SEAS [St. Elizabeth Ann Seton Catholic Church] taught me that what is important is spirituality. We get so wrapped up in our social and humanitarian activities, sometimes, that we forget about our souls. I learned the importance of having a strong spiritual consciousness in our lives... to give people a chance to express their love for Jesus and Mary. This is what it brought me to—a desire to bring Christ to the people in a stronger way.

Q: Do you still get letters from people?

A: Yes, I still get letters and phone calls from people throughout the United States and from foreign countries. Ever so often, someone will drive here from hundreds of miles away. People write to me and say that just hearing about what happened was a conversion experience for them... or they will tell me that just having me write back to them led them back to the Church. People sometimes come here seeking blessings for themselves or their statues or religious medals, rosaries and the like.

Q: Do people still send you rosaries to be blessed?

A: Yes. Sometimes other things, too.

Q: Have your experiences made you a better priest, do you think?

A: Yes, they have. For example, when I preach I always have in the back of my mind the wonderful things that happened at SEAS. That experience has had a tremendous impact upon my sense of the immediate and powerful presence of God and His Blessed Mother. I am always aware now that Jesus can intervene at any time and place when He wishes.

Q: I understand that statues in the rectory at SEAS in the winter and spring of 1993 were exuding oil?

A: Yes, a couple of statues of Mary were doing that for awhile. There were only two statues, one of which was a little Our Lady of Fatima type. [See Figure 3 in the Journal]. It lasted through the Spring of 1993.

Q: Did the oil come from the hands, as I have heard other statues have done?

A: No, It came from the eyes. Instead of water, the statues cried oil for a few months. The oil had the feel, texture and color of olive oil, although I do not know what type of oil it was.

Q: Was exuding oil the last thing that happened?

A: I recall that a little statue wept at my parents' house during Christmas 1994.

Q: Have your stigmata wounds continued to be active?

A: They are not visible anymore and they do not bleed. Once in awhile, I feel the pain. I have noticed that during Holy Week I will usually feel the pains.

Q: Have you ever had any apparitions of the Blessed Virgin Mary or Jesus?

A:	No, not explicitly like some other people have claimed to have. In other words, neither Jesus nor Mary has appeared to me in a visible way so that I could see them with my physical eyes. But, spiritually, I have felt their presence.

Q:	What about other mystical experiences?

A:	At first what I experienced was colors, colors so unique and vivid that I can't really describe them. They weren't really like any colors on earth. After awhile, though, these experiences transitioned into a beautiful sense of the presence of Christ and Mary. Once in awhile this occurs.

Q:	Is there one thing about the whole experience which stands out in your mind?

A:	The conversions. Seeing people come back to Christ has been the most powerful aspect to all the things that happened. There was no explicit message given to me but now, six years later, I see very clearly that truly Christ wanted to bring people back to His Church, to show His closeness to people, to show us His reality. This succeeded, in my opinion. He gave us signs, healings and conversions. And these people who have come back to the Church or renewed their faith have maintained their closeness to Christ. He erased a lot of doubt about His existence and that of His mother, Mary, and the great love which they both have for us.

Q:	Why do you think it happened when and where it did and seemed to be focused upon you?

A:	I have no idea. My own faith was a little shaky at the time, so maybe God decided to use me to reach everyone who felt the way I did. I know I will never have any doubts again. It also had a powerful impact on a lot of people in my family.

Q:	Has Bishop Keating or his Chancellor, Father Rippy, ever brought up this subject? [Bishop Keating died of a heart attack in Rome on March 30, 1998, two and one-half months after this interview first took place.]

A:	No.

AN INTERVIEW WITH FATHER DANIEL HAMILTON

[Father Daniel Hamilton has been the Pastor of Saint Elizabeth Ann Seton Catholic Church since June 1989. This interview took place in his office in May and August 1998.]

Q: Tell me about the first time you learned of the statues weeping.

A: It was December 31, 1991. Father Bruse came into my office and said, "I need to talk to you." He closed the door, sat down, and began to tell me these incredible things. I listened to him with a great deal of skepticism. He could see that I was skeptical so he said that he wanted me to take this one statue which was weeping profusely and see what happened. When he handed it to me, his sleeve pulled back from his wrist and I saw the marks there. That's when I discovered that he had markings like the stigmata.

Q: Which statue did he give you?

A: It was a solid white Fatima statue. I took it from him and put it up in my room. Once there, it began weeping. I moved it to different locations in my room, but no matter where I put it, it wept—so much so that when I put it on my dresser the tears ran down into the drawer! That's when I decided this was not something which I was prepared to handle and told Fr. Bruse that we had to call the bishop.

Q: Did you try to collect any of the tear water? Or notice anything unusual about the tears?

A: No, I didn't try to gather any of the tear water and it appeared to be simply water to me.

Q: I understand that a little statue of Saint Elizabeth Ann Seton wept tears of blood.

A: The only statue which I owned was a small statue of Saint Elizabeth Ann Seton. So I gave that to Fr. Bruse for a few days in exchange for his white Fatima statue. That evening, I noticed in his room that there was red stuff under the eyes.

Q: What did the bishop do with the statues which you took to him?

A:　　He put them in his safe, as I recall. He was going on his vacation the following day.

Q:　　Did you see Fr. Bruse's stigmata wounds bleed?

A:　　Yes, on a couple of occasions. There was blood on his arm when he came to me on January 2 to tell me that the bishop was on the line. It wasn't a lot. I never saw them bleeding heavily, just blood around the marks on his wrists. Later, I noticed stains on my rug which I thought were blood. They did clean up easily, however, so now I'm not sure what they were.

Q:　　How many statues in all do you think you saw weeping?

A:　　Numerous ones—here, in the church, at your house. Maybe a couple of dozen altogether.
　　A classic story I remember in particular took place during a Lenten penance service—an afternoon session for the children (second through fifth graders). We had several priests here to hear confessions. Father George Griffin brought a Mary statue, one of those that looks like it might glow in the dark. He asked Fr. Bruse to bless it and it teared. That caused the penance celebration to get a late start because all of the priests were watching the statue cry.

Q:　　How did Fr. Bruse bless it?

A:　　The same way he usually did—he just held it a moment and gave it back to Fr. Griffin.

Q:　　Considering all the times when you saw statues weeping, is there any possibility that Fr. Bruse could have been "doctoring" them?

A:　　No, none.

Q:　　Did you see a crucifix cry?

A:　　Yes, I saw a crucifix which was hanging on the wall at the diocesan tribunal. It was about a foot or so high. It happened on January 3, following the meeting which Fr. Bruse and I had with the bishop.[1] I needed to stop by the marriage tribunal regarding some cases which I had been handling. Fr. Bruse followed me in and walked down the hallway. As we were leaving he told me the crucifix was crying. I went back to look at it and then I told the secretaries to go and look. Then we left. By the time I returned to SEAS, the phone was ringing. The priest in charge of the tribunal called to say that after our visit they hadn't been able to get any work done! I understand they then called the Chancellor, Monsignor Reinecke, to come down and explain what was going on. He told them that this was a phenomenon which seemed to be associated with Fr. Bruse.

Q: How did Fr. Bruse react to all this phenomena happening around and to him?

A: I think he was as flabbergasted as everyone else. He was obviously mystified by it.

Q: Did Fr. Bruse ever make any suggestion about taking advantage of the weeping statues, etc.?

A: Never, absolutely never! He could have walked away from this a very wealthy man, but he took nothing.

Q: When is the last time you remember seeing any statue weep?

A: My mother came from New Mexico to see a statue weep—it would have been well after Easter 1992. She went into Fr. Bruse's office—he was not there at the time—and that little statue which he keeps in there was tearing.

Q: Were you aware of any testing of the tear water?

A: No.

Q: How would you describe Fr. Bruse's character? Was he like a modern St. Francis of Assisi?

---

[1]There is apparently some confusion in the dates here because this incident was described to me in 1992 as occurring on March 2, and it is reported in the Journal for that date. Six years later it is easy to become confused as to what happened when.

A: Fr. Bruse was a very good priest, a good man. He had his foibles like we all do. He was, without a doubt, the best priest I ever lived with. He was easygoing, easy to get along with, responsible, sociable. He didn't like liquor. I would consider him one of the least pretentious priests I have ever known.

Q: Do you have any ideas about why this all happened around him?

A: Your guess is as good as mine. I have no idea.

Q: Did anyone report miraculous healings to you?

A: No. I occasionally heard others talking about them, but none was reported to me in any official sense.

Q: Did Bishop Keating ever explain to you why he chose not to investigate the weeping statues and other phenomena which were taking place around Father Bruse in 1991 and 1992?

A: He seemed to genuinely believe that an apparition was required to warrant an investigation. [See Appendix A].

Q: To your knowledge, did the diocese do any unofficial investigating of the phenomena?

A: No. It's possible someone from the Chancery might have come down to observe, but no one contacted me in any way. Some priests came by, but they were not representing anyone. Some were friends. Others were just curious.

Q: Did the bishop ever raise the subject at a general meeting with his diocesan clergy?

A: No.

Q: I understand that you gave Bishop Keating a copy of *The Seton Miracles, Weeping Statues and Other Wonders*. Did he make any comments about it to you or to anyone else, to your knowledge?

A: I gave him a copy of the book, as well as the statues which wept and bled from the eyes here. I gave him everything that I had. He never said anything to me about the contents of the book and no one else reported any such comments, either.

Q: Would you say that the bishop, then, kind of implicitly condemned the phenomena?

A: Oh, no. He neither condemned it nor endorsed it. He simply ignored it. He was a very cautious man by nature.

Q: There was a rumor going around when Fr. Bruse was transferred to St. Francis de Sales Church in Kilmarnock that the bishop wanted to get him as far away from the Chancery as possible. Any truth to this?

A: Absolutely none. Fr. Bruse had qualified to become a pastor and St. Francis de Sales was a parish which was coming open in 1995. He wanted a small parish rather than one of the big Northern Virginia ones. From all reports, including Fr. Bruse himself, he has been very happy there.

Q: How would you sum up the whole experience?

A: Those who want to believe, will believe. Those who do not, won't. The results, or fruits, have been very positive. Prior to this happening, we would have only 8...10...12 persons for daily Mass; maybe as high as 15-18 people during Lent. Today, we never have less than 50 persons at daily Mass. That's the first thing.
        The second thing is confessions. Before this happened, one priest could handle the Saturday confessions, which would commonly be only a half dozen or fewer people. When the statues were weeping, we were overwhelmed with people wanting to go to confession. Today, there is still a phenomenal number of confessions every Saturday. We had to move up the starting time to accommodate them. These two spiritual effects alone indicate to me that there was a supernatural origin for all of the phenomena.

AN INTERVIEW WITH MARIE PELLETIER

[Mrs. Marie Pelletier is the Parish Administrator for Saint Elizabeth Ann Seton parish, a position she has held since October 1989. This interview took place in July and August 1998.]

Q: When did you first learn of strange things happening to and around Fr. Bruse?

A: Right after Thanksgiving 1991. Fr. Bruse seemed anxious and a little upset. I could tell there was something he wanted to talk about.

Q: This was very near the beginning of the statues weeping and changing color phenomena. What were your impressions of Fr. Bruse at the time?

A: He seemed very unsure, very scared. He didn't quite know what to think. He had always thought of himself as a simple, basic man and something like this happening to him was very difficult for him. But as time went on, he grew more and more confident as he realized what the message was for him to share.

Q: What was that message?

A: That God is always present; that Jesus is here, among us. We must be prepared for our life after this one on earth.

Q: How did you learn about his stigmata?

A: In early January 1992, he called me into his office. He was bleeding from his wrists, feet and side and was in a tremendous amount of pain. I helped him remove his socks and clean up the blood. It was very humbling for me.

Q: When was the last time you saw Fr. Bruse's stigmata wounds bleed?

A: I'm not sure, but I believe it was during Holy Week in 1995; as I recall, on Good Friday.

Q: When did you first see a religious icon cry?

A: It was right after he told me about what was happening. I remember one time very early on (December 1991) when he was standing in the doorway of his office and suddenly said to me: "Oh, my God!"

I said, "What's happening?" and got up to see. The crucifix that he was touching... there were tears coming out of it, running down the wall, onto the carpeting.

Another time, my oldest son, Christopher, brought one of our family's crucifixes for a blessing and while Christopher was still holding it in his hand it began to cry.

Q: Do you have any idea how many statues you saw weep altogether?

A: Oh, my gosh! It must have been hundreds. People were bringing statues by every day, every day. Father Bruse would bless them all. Sometimes people would just bring bags of statues, pictures in books, everything! A lot of times he would just bless statues in boxes without opening them and the people would walk outside and the box would be wet.

Q: When was the last time you saw a statue weep tears of water?

A: I'm not certain now but even after the statues began to weep oil, they would still occasionally weep tears of water also. So at least it continued well into 1993.

Q: I had heard that some statues were weeping oil in early 1993. Tell me about that phenomenon. For example, which statues exuded oil? Did it come from the hands, too, or only the eyes?

A: I recall just two statues which wept oil. They were Fr. Bruse's personal statues which he kept in his office. One of them was the little Our Lady of Grace statue [see Figure 1]. This is the one I saw. The other, I believe, was a Fatima statue. There may have been others but I didn't see them.

The oil always came out of the eyes, never the hands. It was very light and clear for an oil—not heavy at all. It was lighter than chrism oil. Sometimes it had a very sweet fragrance; sometimes it had no fragrance at all.

Q: Did you keep any of the oil?

A: I dabbed it up with some cloths and I do have those still.

Q: Did you see rosaries change color?

A: Yes. People would ask Fr. Bruse to bless them. He would hold the rosary (ies) in one hand and cup the other one over them and say a blessing. When he removed his hand, frequently the rosaries would have changed color. Silver rosaries would become gold; crystal rosaries would become red or blue.

Q: How many rosaries did you see this happen to?

A: Maybe twenty or so. Some of these rosaries came in the mail. Fr. Bruse would bless it, it would change color, and then we would mail it back to the person who sent it.

Q: During the height of the weeping phenomena, there were thousands of "pilgrims" and visitors to the church. They came to see the Our Lady of Smiles statue, which was the only Madonna statue permanently placed in the church and the most accessible when it wept, and to see Fr. Bruse and receive his blessing. Were you receiving a lot of correspondence during this time?

A: Oh, yes! Besides rosaries, people sent us their little statues, complete with return postage and address labels. Thousands of letters came in. To his credit, Fr. Bruse answered every letter, every single one!

Q: What about the press?

A: Oh, they were constantly calling. I often had the impression, though, that they already had their stories written and were just looking for quotes which would support their point of view. From this standpoint, the bishop's decision to ignore the weeping statues and other phenomena probably helped us. Because we were not supposed to encourage or facilitate their reporting, we had fewer problems with false and misleading reports.

Q: Did Bishop Keating or anyone from the Diocese of Arlington try to help any of you manage the situation?

A: No. The Chancery left us completely alone. It was very hard sometimes. There were a lot of rumors flying around then but I was unable to comment. I felt a very strong loyalty to Fr. Bruse... to not betray his trust and confidence in me.

Q: Did you see any statues bleed?

A: I didn't see any while they were bleeding but I did see one afterwards. That was the little Saint Elizabeth Ann Seton statue which Fr. Hamilton exchanged with Fr. Bruse on New Year's Eve.

Q: Did you ever see a statue change its colors?

A: Yes. The first time was around Christmas in 1991. I had this big (about 24") Our Lady of Grace statue which I brought in for Fr. Bruse to bless. I put it on his desk and it began to weep profusely—the water was just coming down and there were puddles all around the base! I called Dick [her husband] to bring all my linen handkerchiefs. By the time he arrived, the statue had stopped crying and he tried very hard to figure out where all that water might have come from—without it being a miracle!

Before Dick arrived, the statue also began to add and change its colors. The inside of Mary's robe turned from white to pink and the outside blue of the robe went from a faded color into a deep blue.

You wrote about the little Fatima statue weeping in the psychiatrist's office in January 1992. I had accompanied Fr. Bruse on that trip and when we were coming home we opened the box in which he had carried the statue. As it lay there, it was changing colors—and not just any colors. They were like colors I had never seen: incredibly vibrant blues, greens, pinks. The change was slow—one color would slowly be replaced by another one. This lasted about 20-30 minutes.

I also remember seeing statues which came into Fr. Bruse's office which were all white at first and then took on various colors in their robes.

Q: Did you observe any statue animation?

A: No.

Q: Did you observe any inexplicable healings?

A: No, but I did hear of them. I know, for example, of people who came with cancerous tumors to see Fr. Bruse and, after he had blessed them, would return to their doctors to discover that the tumors had vanished.

Q: I know that many of the reportedly miraculous healings involved people who are apparently unwilling to share the stories of their cures. Why is that?

A: I don't know. Fr. Bruse was concerned about their privacy and possible hounding by the press. Some of the people themselves were afraid of the consequences of publicity for their families. And we had so many other very public miracles that this just didn't seem necessary to be disclosed since its personal impact is so great. People who were looking for evidence of God's presence in our lives had an overwhelming number of signs without adding the healing stories.

You have to remember, too, that Bishop Keating had requested the priests not to do anything to promote people's interest in seeing these phenomena or coming to SEAS in hopes of gaining a miracle for themselves. Certainly if we had encouraged people to publish their miraculous healing stories, we would have produced a deluge of visitors seeking similar benefits. Fr. Bruse never thought of himself as having this particular charisma. It was the Holy Spirit working through him. The healings that occurred seemed to be accompaniments to all the other phenomena which were taking place.

Q: What about the "miracle of the sun," meaning the ability to look directly at it and see it spinning and/or throwing off colors, etc.? Did you have this experience?

A: Yes, nearly every day. I would see a kind of circle over the sun—a deep, almost indescribable golden disk. Then slowly the sun would begin to spin and, as it did, it would fill the whole sky with beautiful colors. Two times I saw the sun spinning surrounded by red. Other times I would see it surrounded by the color blue. Sometimes it pulsated like a beating heart.

Q: Was there any particular time of day when this would occur? Did you see it every time you looked at the sun?

A: It happened all different times of the day but not every time I looked toward the sun. When the sun sign was there, I would get this feeling—sort of like a spiritual tapping on my shoulder with an invitation to "Look up."

Q: Did anyone else see this at the time?

A: I did call some people sometimes and tell them to look up at the sun [see p. 63 of the Journal]. One time I was walking with my husband, Dick, and I suddenly had the feeling come over me. I asked Dick if he could see the sign but he could not.

Q: Do you still see this sign?

A: Yes.

Q: Fr. Bruse's mystical experiences are quite remarkable—reminiscent of some near death experience (NDE) reports in their description of an overpowering sense of love from a beautiful heavenly figure and the appearance of a reality far more intense and vivid than that which we experience on earth. But, as I understand it, he never saw anything more specific; i.e., he never had an apparition of the Blessed Virgin Mary or Jesus, like those reported from Medjugorje, Fatima and Lourdes. What do you know about this?

A: There were no apparitions but there were times when the feeling of a "Presence" was so strong that you knew it, you could feel it with every part of your body. You just knew there was a Presence there. You could feel this Presence come and be a part of Fr. Bruse and then leave.

Q: Can you describe a specific instance of this?

A: The one I remember especially was during the SEAS Festival [May 1992]. Fr. Bruse and I were sitting outside under one of the tents. It was raining. I could see the pain in his face and when I looked down I could see that he was bleeding. So we got up and went back to his office in the rectory.
         All at once my heart began to beat much faster and Fr. Bruse looked at me and said, "There's a Presence in this room."
          It was incredible—so beautiful! Peace, beauty love, mercy, hope—it was like everything wrapped into one magnificent feeling.

Q: Did you notice any other indications of this Presence, such as fragrances, light, etc.?

A: There was a faint scent of roses. I had smelled this fragrance before, more noticeably, but this was the strongest "Presence" I had ever experienced.

Q: How did Fr. Bruse react?

A: Very comfortably, like he was completely familiar with the experience. I believe he felt it was the Blessed Virgin Mary who was present with us.

STATUE WEEPINGS AROUND THE WORLD

Our Lady's tears belong to the order of signs: they testify to the presence of the Mother in the Church and in the world.—Pope John Paul II at the dedication of the Shrine of Our Lady of Tears.

Although there has been no reported weeping display anywhere in the world or throughout history to equal that which occurred in and around Lake Ridge with Father Bruse as the catalyst, there have been innumerable other weepings in this country and in many other nations. Father Albert J. Hebert, S.M., provides comprehensive summaries of these weepings, including dozens of photographs, in his two books, *The Tears of Mary—and Fatima, Why?*, and *Mary, Why Do You Cry?* Both books are generally available in Catholic bookstores and can be ordered directly from the author at P.O. Box 309, Paulina, LA 70763.

I will not repeat what Father Hebert has so thoroughly detailed, except to note that the weepings and bleedings from statues about which he reports take place in Italy (many—of both tears and blood), Belgium, Ireland, Egypt, Colombia, Chile, India, South Korea, Philippines, Lebanon, Syria, Japan, Vietnam, South Korea, Canada, Poland, Syria, France, Haiti, Spain and China. Weepings have also been reported in England, Mexico, Puerto Rico, Trinidad and Australia.

In the United States, Fr. Hebert describes numerous weepings in locations all around the country, usually involving a Fatima statue, such as the North American Pilgrim Virgin Fatima statue or the International Pilgrim Virgin Fatima statue. Another type of Madonna statue which has wept frequently is the Rosa Mystica. Some of the places where these weepings occurred include Louisiana, Nevada, Washington, D.C. (a precursor!), New York, Georgia, Pennsylvania and Illinois. In addition, there have been reports of weepings in Texas, California, Ohio, Kansas and Massachusetts in the past few years.

Statues weeping seems to be largely a 20th Century phenomenon. Given the barbarities which the human race has inflicted upon itself in this century, this is somehow not surprising. But, ominously, the tears may have less to do with the destruction of lives than the loss of souls, as we shall see in the chapter, "What Does It All Mean?"

Perhaps the most famous weeping in Church history took place in the very modest home of a newly-married Italian couple in Syracuse, Sicily, in 1953. The young couple was poor, expecting their first child in about four months, and struggling economically. Their home was located in a rundown section known as "Hell Row." It began on Saturday, August 29, 1953, at 8:30 in the morning. Antonina Giusto-Jannuso, suffering from an odd illness which produced convulsions and temporary blindness, was lying in bed. She had had one of her seizures at 3:00 a.m. that same morning and now awoke wondering if convulsions would follow as they often had. As she lay there, her gaze rose to the wall above her to a glazed plaster bas-relief of a Madonna statue portraying the Immaculate Heart of Mary. The image was mounted on a black, curved glass background.

"The Madonna—look, the Madonna is weeping!" screamed Antonina as she realized that tears were forming and dripping from both eyes of the little 12-inch figure. Soon other members of the family had gathered to witness the steady flow of tears, now falling on the headboard of the bed. Neighbors were invited to watch the weeping and the crowd grew steadily throughout the day. Angelo Jannuso, Antonina's husband, came home from work at 5:30 p.m. and watched the tears fall a half hour later.

By 9:00 p.m., the crowd was threatening the ability of the police to control it. They confiscated the Madonna plaque and took it to police headquarters for examination. They removed the back and examined the plaster. It was hollow and dry and the police determined that the weeping was, indeed, coming only from the eyes. After forty minutes, Angelo Jannuso was allowed to take the little figure home. He hid it in first one brother's house, then another's. A few hours later, at 2:00 a.m., the Madonna image was taken to No. 11, Via degli Orti. It was weeping and was placed on a cushion. The family slept awhile then slipped away to the countryside while it was still dark to escape the crowd. But the police tracked them down and asked them to return to Syracuse and open the house so the people could view the image. That afternoon, Sunday, August 30, the Madonna plaque was placed on a table in the house at No. 11, Via degli Orti. The crowd filed in through that house and exited through an adjoining home at No. 9.

The next day, Monday the 31st of August, the statue was displayed outside the house. Thousands of people from all over Italy converged on the little street. Throughout the day, the statue wept as the crowd filed by, touching and drying the tears. At 9:00 p.m. it was taken back to the Jannuso home.

At 11:00 a.m. on September 1, 1953, a medical commission sent by the Archbishop's Curia of Syracuse arrived at the Jannuso house to gather some of the tear water for analysis. They were able to collect about thirty drops worth. At 11:40 a.m., the Madonna stopped weeping for good.

The investigation determined that there was no natural explanation for the weeping and that the water which was coming from the eyes had the composition of real human tears. Accordingly, on December 11, 1953, the Bishops of Sicily declared "the reality of the weeping cannot be held in doubt." In Rome a week later, the *Osservatore Romano* declared: "They (the Bishops) have expressed the

Figure 13. *Shrine of Our Lady of Tears, Syracuse, Sicily*
Capacity: 11,000 people

sincere desire that this manifestation of our heavenly Mother may inspire the whole world with a true spirit of penance, and more fervent devotion to the Immaculate Heart of Mary. It is likewise their wish that a spiritual edifice be erected to commemorate the miracle."[1]

Forty-one years later, on November 6, 1994, the great basilica—the Shrine of Our Lady of Tears—was dedicated by His Holiness, Pope John Paul II. In his dedication homily, the Pope categorized the tears of Madonna images:

> "These are *tears of sorrow* for all those who refuse the love of God, for those families who are broken or in difficulty, for the young people seduced by a consumerist civilization and so often disorientated, for the violence that still spills so much blood and for the misunderstandings and hate which dig deep trenches between individuals and peoples.
>
> "They are *tears of prayer:* the Mother's prayer that gives strength to every other prayer, and that rises in supplication for all those who do not pray because they are distracted by a thousand other interests, or because they are obstinately closed to God's call.
>
> "They are *tears of hope,* which melt the hardness of hearts and open them to meeting Christ the Redeemer, source of light and peace for individuals, for families, for the whole of society."

Twenty years after Syracuse, the Blessed Virgin Mary manifested herself in an even more dramatic fashion in a convent of nuns, Servants of the Eucharist, dedicated to adoration of the Holy Eucharist, in Akita, Japan. Sister Agnes Sasagawa was one of the residents of this convent, a woman who had suffered several medical crises in her life and had recently lost all her hearing. On June 12, 1973, the 42 year old nun saw a brilliant white light burst forth from the tabernacle when she opened it. After encounters with the Blessed Virgin Mary and her guardian angel, by July 6, Sr. Agnes had received a bleeding stigmata wound in her left hand in the form of a cross. The next day, the same wound appeared in the right hand of a statue of the Blessed Virgin Mary representing Our Lady of All Nations (the statue was also known as the Virgin of Akita). Blood flowed from the statue's wound but never fell to the ground. This went on for three weeks, finally ending on July 27, 1973.

---

[1]Hebert, *The Tears of Mary—and Fatima,Why?,* p. 49.

On September 29, 1973, the statue began to perspire heavily, especially from the forehead and neck. The entire statue was soaked. A beautiful fragrance accompanied the sweat.

The statue wept for the first time on January 4, 1975, a First Friday. Sr. Agnes' guardian angel explained the purpose of the weeping to be a visible sign for people of weak faith of the Blessed Mother's desire for the conversion of souls. Noting that even the local pastor at that time was afraid to come to the convent for fear of what people might think, she offered this visible sign to embolden those who seek reassurance.

The statue wept for the last time, the 101st weeping, on September 15, 1981, the Feast of Our Lady of Sorrows. During the six years of the statue's periodic tearing, it was seen by local city officials and on Japanese television, broadcast to millions. Hundreds of others, believers and unbelievers alike, saw the statue weep in person.

Two weeks later, on September 28, 1981, Sr. Agnes' guardian angel explained to her the meaning of the 101 weepings. The first "one" represents Eve, by whom sin came into the world. The second "one" signifies the woman (Mary) by whom salvation came into the world. The zero in between represents the Eternal God who exists from all eternity. Sr. Agnes was also shown a passage from the Bible, Genesis 3:15, which is considered the first prophecy of God's redemption of mankind.

On Easter Sunday, April 22, 1984, the Most Reverend John Ito, Bishop of Niigata, officially declared the events of Akita to be supernatural. Father Yasuda, Sr. Agnes' spiritual director, reported that samples of the statue's tears, blood and sweat were sent to the Laboratory of Akita University for analysis on separate occasions. The blood typed as B and the sweat as AB the first time. The next time, nearly three years later, the sweat typed as O. Father Yasuda believes the variation was intended by God to refute any suggestion that the blood and sweat came from Sr. Agnes.

In a television interview in Japan, the woodcarver of the statue of Our Lady of Akita expressed astonishment that the wood of the statue changed color only for the face, hands and feet (a brownish red) and declared that it was impossible for the Katsura wood out of which the statue was carved to shed water.

Father Jim Bruse's stigmata wounds, now invisible but still manifesting themselves periodically, and the incredible display of weeping statues and other phenomena which took place around him, were not accompanied by personal apparitions as at Akita. Perhaps one of the reasons for this is that the Blessed Mother had already expressed herself clearly enough and saw no need to repeat her entreaties. Before we leave Akita, then, let us consider her words on July 12, 1973:

> "My daughter, do you love the Lord? If you love Him, please listen to what I say to you. Inform your superior of my request. In the world, many people afflict the Lord. I seek souls to console Him. To assuage the sorrow of the Eternal Father at His children's disobedience, which gives rise to His mighty justice, I, with my Son, await those souls who will expiate with their suffering and their spirit of renunciation for these sins of ingratitude. My Son and I unite with us generous souls as a gift to our Father.
>
> "The Eternal Father is quite prepared to allow the world's peoples to experience the consequences of their spirit of disobedience and rebellion to His Divine Plan. I with my Son have often intervened in the affairs of the world to mollify the natural justice of God which allows humanity to bear the consequences of their own choices. Our intervention has delayed the calamities that people have created for one another and for the planet. My Son offers all His suffering on the Cross, along with mine, and all the victim souls who unite their sufferings and penances to God as a gift of love.
>
> "Prayer, penance, courageous sacrifice mitigate the consequences of evil behavior. I ask your community to live in strict poverty so that the ingratitude and outrages of many may be touched by your spirit of reparation. As you recite the Prayer of the Servants of the Eucharist be fully conscious of its meaning. Put it into practice and offer it in reparation for sins. Ask everyone in the entire world, according to their position, to say this prayer as a sin offering. Offer yourselves entirely to the Lord."[2]

---

[2]Here is the prayer referred to by the Blessed Mother: "*Most Sacred Heart of Jesus, truly present in the Holy Eucharist, I consecrate my body and soul to be entirely one with Your Heart being sacrified at every instant on all the altars of the world, and giving praise to the Father, pleading for the Coming of His Kingdom. Please receive this humble offering of myself. Use me as You will for the glory of the Father and the salvation of souls. Amen*" And also: "*Lord Jesus Christ, Son of the Father, send Your Spirit over the earth. Make Your Spirit dwell in the hearts of all the people that they will be delivered from corruption, disasters and war. Amen.*"

Three months later, on October 13, 1973, the anniversary of the miracle of the sun at Fatima, Sr. Agnes again heard a voice seeming to come from the statue:

> "Listen carefully to what I say to you and inform your superior. If humanity does not repent and improve, the Eternal Father will allow a terrible punishment to befall all humankind. This punishment will be worse than the flood or any that has ever been seen before. A fire will fall from the sky and annihilate large numbers. Neither priests nor the faithful will be spared. The survivors will be in such desolation that they will envy the dead.
>
> "The only weapons that will remain will be the Rosary and the Sign that the Eternal Father will leave. Pray the Rosary every day. The devil's attack will be the most intense against those who have consecrated themselves to God.
>
> "The loss of so many souls will deepen the grievous sorrow in my heart. If sins grow and become more accepted there will be no pardon for them."[3]

This is the message of Fatima, approved by the Church. This is the message of Akita, approved by the Church. This is surely the message of Lake Ridge, even though the Church has not yet addressed the origins and significance of that remarkable outburst of weeping statues near our nation's capital.

In Civitavecchia, Italy, in early February, 1995, an eighteen-inch tall plaster statue of Our Lady of Medjugorje began to weep tears of blood, according to the parish priest and the statue's owner. The news created a sensation in this small port city of 50,000 people forty miles north of Rome as soon as it was announced. Similar phenomena were reported in about a dozen other Italian towns. In response to the great public interest and the attendant controversy, Bishop Grillo took custody of the statue and kept it in his home for awhile.

Then the police got involved and ordered DNA testing of the dried blood. The tests showed the blood to be from a human male. Neither the owner of the statue and his family, nor the parish priest, were willing to submit blood samples

---

[3]These quotes and the ones on the previous page are taken from *Meetings with Mary, Visions of the Blessed Mother*, by Janice T. Connell, New York:Ballantine Books, 1995, pp. 136-139.

for DNA comparison, saying they feared an official conspiracy to discredit the phenomena. Father Pablo Martin, the priest, also said that his refusal was to protest police investigations of religious phenomena.

Bishop Grillo has restored the statue to its niche at San Agostino Catholic Church. He is noncommittal about the nature of the weeping, calling it a "wondrous event" but avoiding use of the word "miracle." Certainly some of his hesitation is probably attributable to the eager plans of city fathers to exploit the phenomenon for economic gain. *Newsweek* magazine responded with an irreverent blurb in its March 27, 1995, issue trivializing the bleeding icon by suggesting it might be weeping because of Italy's soccer loss in the World Cup matches.

The Civitavecchia incident is a good one for illustrating the need for impartial discernment. That situation has elements which are difficult to sort out in trying to determine whether there is fraud involved, or whether the bleeding is a genuine supernatural sign. The lesson for us is to use the good sense which God gave us, but not to fall prey to the agenda of the faithless and worldly who are the declared enemies of any supernatural claim. Examine the evidence carefully. Test it, as Saint Paul advised.[4] Form your judgments based on the facts. But keep an open mind and remember that suspicion, innuendo and slanderous or mocking accusations speak volumes about their proponents but say nothing about a specific phenomenon.

In Worcester, Massachusetts, a 14-year old girl lies in a coma from which she has not recovered since a near-drowning at age three. Her name is Audrey Santo. Around her, numerous religious icons of the Blessed Virgin Mary and Jesus weep oil. Eucharistic wafers have been said to bleed and chalices have suddenly filled with fragrant oil, smelling powerfully of roses. Some have reported statues moving on their own. There have been claims of miraculous healings. This has been going on for more than four years. Audrey's former doctor states unequivocally that as far as cognitive functions are concerned, Audrey is dead. Her only brain activity resides in the physical body functions controlled by the brain stem.[5]

The Mercy Foundation has produced a one-hour video, titled *Audrey's Life: Voice of a Silent Soul*. In it, a priest holds up a Communion Host and is

---

[4] 1Thes 5:21

[5] The facts presented here regarding Audrey Santo are drawn from an article which appeared in *The Washington Post* in the Style section on July 19, 1998, titled, "Tears for Audrey."

astonished to see that it has a wet red spot on it in the shape of a cross. Subsequent tests revealed the red liquid to be human blood.

As might be expected, there are several opinions as to the meaning of Audrey's remarkably good health, considering her circumstances, and the apparently miraculous phenomena surrounding her. A priest suggests that the miraculous signs point to the evils of abortion and birth control. A physician says her survival and the signs which envelop her now condemn physician-assisted suicide, and testify to the value of all life and the dignity in suffering. Others assert that Audrey is a "victim soul," voluntarily assuming the symptoms of others with serious illnesses as a sign of her spiritual alertness, charity and willingness to bear these sufferings in the spirit of Christ. Another priest rejects the notion that Audrey could be a victim soul, seeing in that too harsh a treatment by God of an innocent child. He believes she represents a divine reminder to us that killing is wrong, pointing out that her accident occurred on the anniversary of the nuclear bombing of Nagasaki (August 9th).

The diocese of Worcester has appointed an investigative commission, headed by a nonclerical psychotherapist. The investigation is not concluded yet, but the psychotherapist has already reported seeing inexplicable signs involving religious icons.

For our purposes, what conclusions might we draw from the Audrey Santo experience? It is worth noting, by the way, that her family is reported to be very much down-to-earth, no nonsense, accepting of the presence of God in their daily lives, possessing a sense of humor and grounded in the realities of blue collar life in America. Audrey has not been exploited in any way for her financial possibilities. In this sense, they sound much like lay versions of Fr. Bruse, who is also straightforward, likable, and normal in his role as pastor of his Catholic parish, and who also avoided any attempt to profit from the mysterious signs which surrounded him at Lake Ridge.

A few conclusions about Audrey Santo seem obvious. Under very adverse circumstances that every right-to-die proponent would undoubtedly consider more than sufficient justification to terminate her life with euthanasia, God sends miracles to tell us that He values her life. The tears that flow from religious icons around Audrey are tears of oil, not water, a substance which is associated with sickness and healing. As with all such miraculous signs, conversions and a renewed faith in God are the primary and most important fruits. These abound. The periodic manifestations in Audrey's body of the symptoms of other people suffering from serious illness suggest that all of us can help others by sharing in their sufferings. This is just a practical twist on a well-accepted spiritual doctrine that victim souls who bear their sufferings for love of Christ and humanity help to atone for the sins of all. As to whether the unconscious Audrey bears her sufferings voluntarily, I think we would have to conclude that either she is unconscious of those sufferings or she certainly bears them voluntarily because her soul is cognizant and present to the supernatural reality of Jesus and the Blessed Virgin Mary. I favor the latter conclusion. But, either way, one could not legitimately accuse God of being a "monster" if He allows Audrey to voluntarily suffer as an apparent victim soul.

I suggest that the primary message of Audrey Santo's miraculous signs may be that God is the source of our healing and that He will be there for us when we finally acknowledge that He is real, present to us in our everyday lives, and seek His forgiveness and grace. Through Audrey, and the symbolism of oil, which is used to anoint in the Sacrament of the Sick, we are reminded of Christ's redemptive suffering and the immense spiritual value that suffering can have in atoning for our own sins and the sins of others. As the Blessed Virgin Mary explained to the children of Fatima:

> "Pray, pray very much, and make sacrifices for sinners; for many souls go to hell because there are none to sacrifice themselves and to pray for them."[6]

In summary, then, the tears of the Blessed Virgin Mary represent at least three concepts. First, the tears of water are the tears of a mother weeping for her children who are in extremely grave danger. Second, the tears of blood remind us of the terrible price Christ paid for our salvation, as well as the sufferings of His Blessed Mother who stood at the foot of His cross, and may also include a warning of catastrophes threatening mankind. Third, the tears of oil are reassurance that the Holy Mother of God is anxious to console us and to help us. She longs to bind up the wounds to our souls and restore us to spiritual health, if we will but turn to her and to her Son and ask for His pardon and grace to amend our lives.

---

[6]*Fatima in Lucia's Own Words*, ed. Fr. Louis Kondor, SVD, Cambridge, MA: Ravensgate Press, 1976, p. 167, from the August 1917 apparition.

A REPLY TO THE SKEPTICS

[T]hey will not be convinced even if one should rise from the dead. Lk 16:31

      Skepticism is not a bad thing. Saint Paul himself maintained a healthy skepticism and his advice to us is, "Test everything; retain what is good." (1Thes 5:21). But skepticism should not be confused with cynicism. And skepticism plus willful ignorance often equal stupidity.

      Religion is all about faith... and love. Faith is an integral part of God's design for the salvation of mankind. It is not a negative thing, referring to what's left after we have exhausted all the empirical data available to our rational minds. It is a positive element that opens our hearts to God's grace. It is the vehicle which transports us to a closer relationship with God. It is our spiritual currency and those blessed with great faith are rich, indeed. As Jesus told Saint Thomas after His resurrection:

> "You became a believer because you saw me. Blest are they who
> have not seen and have believed." Jn 20:29

      So in this sense, it is perhaps a misnomer to characterize those of us who witnessed statues weeping inexplicable tears and other miraculous phenomena as being blessed because such signs and wonders are really intended for the weak of faith, the confused, the doubtful, the nonbelievers. Still, the struggle to hold onto religious beliefs in a skeptical, neo-pagan world can be hard and so a little boost to our faith is almost always greatly appreciated. We who were at Saint Elizabeth Ann Seton Catholic Church in 1992-93 had an overwhelming quantity of miraculous signs for which to be grateful. Through such means as this book, we are able to share the blessing with those who were not here or did not experience any of the miraculous phenomena. This chapter addresses some of the challenges to these signs so that those who have open minds can rest assured that what is reported here unmistakably came from God.

      But, be careful, too. Miracles do not replace faith. Faith is necessary to our salvation. It is the soil for the love which God will plant in our souls, love which will be the fruit that we will harvest in everlasting happiness with Him. Miracles only serve to get and hold our attention. They are motivators to embrace and live our faith with conviction and confidence. They do not in any way substitute for the need to grow in our faith by means of Scripture; the Sacraments, especially the Eucharist and confession; frequent prayer; and good works. If you are unable to distinguish the real Mother of God from her statues, whether they wept and changed colors, smiled, or not, you have already missed the point. These things were a beautiful, engraved invitation from God. Treasure the invitation, but focus on the banquet to which you have been invited.

You should understand, too, that the secular world is often the avowed enemy of the spiritual kingdom. Do not expect neutrality and unbiased opinions. In the secular world, man is worshipped for his reason and technological prowess. God and all things supernatural are dismissed as the invention of unsophisticated minds or the byproduct of a death-haunted, anxiety-ridden mankind. These are the views of the faithless. Do not assume they are knowledgeable, for they are often grossly ignorant. They are blind and deaf to supernatural reality. Or, at best, they are more than willing to draw conclusions which discredit the supernatural on the basis of entirely erroneous information. For example, in a July 19, 1998 article in *The Washington Post*, titled "Tears for Audrey," Gene Weingarten wrote the following:

> "But mostly, in these cases, one is left with proof of nothing, only a feeling of unease: An obscure priest in a Lake Ridge, Va., parish briefly became a national celebrity in 1992 when figurines began crying in his presence. Was he a faker? Maybe, maybe not. Journalists discovered that, as a young man, he had once sought a sort of wacko fame by riding for days nonstop in a roller coaster. Soon after this was published, the figurines dried up. Eventually, the priest was moved to another parish. End of story."

It seems a bit arrogant to suggest that journalists' discovery of Fr. Bruse's world record in nonstop roller coaster riding had anything to do with the inexplicable weeping of religious icons.[1] Or, more darkly, it is a subtle accusation of fraud by Fr. Bruse that was discouraged by this "exposé." Either way, Weingarten has his facts wrong. The report about Fr. Bruse's roller coaster exploits was published by the *Post*, complete with photo, in a March 13, 1992, story titled "The Weeping Statues of the Bleeding Priest." Not only did the weeping not stop soon after this story was published, but the number and frequency of inexplicable phenomena *increased* and reached an ever-widening circle of people. It went on for more than a year after this story was published.

---

[1]Fr. Bruse was well-compensated for this feat, which was part of a Kings Dominion promotional campaign. He also participated for purposes of raising funds for charity.

Other equally befuddled commentators have suggested that because statues can be made to weep by artificial means, that the phenomenon automatically falls into the category of pseudo-religion, fraud and/or superstition. By this logic, please ignore the next person you see weeping, even if it is your spouse (this might be perilous to you) or other family member, because since actors can fake tears, no one can be believed to be genuinely sorrowful. Also, applying the same logic, suggest to such persons that they turn over to you all the currency in their wallets because, since money can be counterfeited, no currency can be accepted as real.

Another example of misleading secular comment about the significance of weeping statues can be found in a review of *The Demon-Haunted World,* a book by the late Carl Sagan. This review by Martin Gardner appeared in *The Washington Post's* "Book World" section on March 17, 1996. Mr. Gardner, who had high praise for this work by Sagan, reported: "Other follies covered by Sagan include...bleeding and weeping statues of the Virgin Mary;" Well, okay, let's see what Dr. Sagan has to tell us. Perhaps he, of all people, can unlock the mystery of how statues can be made to weep under the circumstances surrounding Father Bruse. On page 209 of *Demon-Haunted World* we discover that Dr. Sagan's *total* coverage of this phenomenon consists of the following sentence: *"Statues of Jesus or murals of Mary are spotted with moisture, and thousands of kind-hearted people convince themselves that they have witnessed a miracle."* He adds: *"These are all cases of proved or presumptive baloney."*[2] Now there's the "scientific method" at work for you. No hypotheses, no facts, no analysis—only unsupported conclusions.

But do not assume that the religious press is any better. Go back and read the preface to this book, pp. xiv-xv, for another shining example of confident condemnation completely unencumbered by any actual facts.

When you follow the Apostle Paul's advice to test everything, be sure that you gather the facts before you start the testing process, unlike these so-called experts.

Q: In the past, there have been instances of religious fraud involving statues which were chemically treated or rigged to weep water or oil. How can we be sure that the events surrounding Father Bruse were not also fraudulent?

---

[2]Besides weeping statues, Sagan is referring to such dubious practices as psychic surgery, psychic investigation of crime, and airborne dowsing rods to find mineral deposits.

A: Statues, even paintings, can be made to weep with chemicals. This has been demonstrated numerous times. The fake tear water can even be made to taste salty. Other frauds have involved using materials which react to changes in temperature to produce some form of liquefaction. If a statue is large enough, or there is available space behind a picture, mechanical devices can be used to deliver water through the surface of the image.

But all of these fraudulent techniques require manipulation. One must have access and means to set up the trick. In the case of Father Bruse, he often did not have such access. For example, Tom Saunders took a bagful of statues to Fr. Bruse to be blessed on January 26, 1992, and never removed them from their towel wrappings. When he returned home, most of the towels were wet from the weeping by the little Madonna figures. Pinkey Carney observed statues weeping on March 24, 1992, while being held by people waiting in line for Fr. Bruse to bless them. The Journal included in this book is full of instances where statues, crucifixes and images wept despite not being touched by Fr. Bruse. A Madonna bust in a glass-enclosed cabinet at my house in a room where Fr. Bruse did not even enter wept on St. Patrick's Day, 1992.

Furthermore, merely touching a statue cannot make it weep. Try it yourself. In more than a year of careful observation under all kinds of circumstances and conditions, not one person *ever* reported seeing Fr. Bruse doing anything suspicious with his hands or acting in any way as if he had doctored a statue.

The number of statues which wept is also incompatible with any fraudulent scheme. Altogether, probably hundreds of these little images shed tears before thousands of witnesses. The ability to manipulate a single statue or image is one thing. But no one could have begun to manage the huge number of religious icons which manifested miraculous physical displays, such as weeping, changing color, and becoming animated.

Finally, those who engage in fraud do so for a motive, usually financial. In this case, there has not been a single suggestion of any financial profiteering by Fr. Bruse or anyone else associated with the phenomena. Nor was there any effort to encourage visits by "pilgrims," whose contributions would have aided the parish's building plans. On the contrary, their presence was discouraged in accordance with the Chancery's statement (see Appendix A) and the bishop's admonition to Fathers Hamilton and Bruse. Even *The Washington Post* in its April

5, 1992, article, "Treading Softly Into the Matter of Miracles," questioned the credence of such an accusation for a rapidly-growing, prosperous parish.[3]

Q: Couldn't there be some natural explanation for the phenomena; some strange circumstance which we don't fully understand?

A: No known set of physical conditions could have produced the phenomena which occurred to and around Fr. Bruse. Humidity might cause generalized "sweating" in certain physical objects, but never localized in one tiny part of the object, such as the eyes. Further, the weeping occurred at all times of the day and evening, in many different temperature conditions. Before the phenomena started and since they ended, these same objects in the same conditions have never manifested anything out of the ordinary.

Only religious items displayed the inexplicable activity. If the effect is exclusively religious, it stands to reason that the cause is religious, too.

Finally, to posit the notion that Fr. Bruse was somehow causing these things to happen by means of some subconscious paranormal power unknown even to himself is simply preposterous.

Q: Some commentators have suggested that the statues were not really weeping and that the reports of tears were simply the product of crowd hysteria and reflected light.

A: See the photos in this book. Cameras are not hysterical nor influenced by psychological factors. Do the tears depicted in these photos look to you like tricks of lighting? The dozens of witnesses who contributed to this book were all normal, well-balanced members of the community, leading successful lives in challenging careers and/or raising families. There was not a single news report or even a suggestion of public hysteria during any statue phenomenon.

Q: Joe Nickell is a professional "debunker" and has written a book titled *Looking for a Miracle, Weeping Icons, Relics, Stigmata, Visions & Healing Cures.* Doesn't he pretty well undermine Fr. Bruse and the Lake Ridge weepings?

A: Let's take a look. To start, Nickell discusses the famous Syracuse, Italy weeping which took place August 29 - September 1, 1953, and was pronounced

---

[3]Metro Section, p. B5.

worthy of belief by the faithful as being a probable miracle. This proclamation was based upon a prompt and thorough investigation and analysis by the archdiocese in Sicily which had jurisdiction. [See the chapter on "Statue Weepings Around the World" in this book]. Nickell hints that the investigators could not be trusted and concludes, to the extent that the weeping is inexplicable, it was probably caused by a "limited form of poltergeist attack." There it is again: somehow, the affected person has amazing, subconscious powers they do not even know they have; or, maybe we have a minor league devil acting up. Any possibility is acceptable except the obvious one: God wishing to send a very meaningful message to us through an image of His Blessed Mother. Nickell goes on to describe the events, rhetoric dripping with scorn and hints of chicanery, but fails to produce any factual basis to question the church determination in that case. He makes liberal use of the "guilt by association" technique by describing other Italian weepings which were less authenticated, calling them "an epidemic of imitative miracles." Through his cynical, tunnel vision, these multiple weepings are evidence of deception. But from God's perspective, it is a natural and effective way of making sure His message is received.

Nickell cites four possible causes for statues weeping, other than the possibility of a genuine supernatural cause, of course. These are condensation, deliberate hoaxing, imagination and illusion. You don't need me to address these. Go back and read the Journal again. Check out the photos. Remember, too, that two of Father Bruse's little statues can be seen weeping in the first television news broadcast back on March 6, 1992. And *The Washington Post* reporter saw, touched and tasted statue tears which fell from the figure's eyes for the story which appeared on March 13, 1992 ("The Weeping Statues of the Bleeding Priest"). So much for condensation, imagination and illusion.

For Nickell, deliberate hoaxing includes chemical and mechanical means, but he offers very few details for either technique, mentioning only calcium chloride for chemistry and quickly jumping to such preposterous techniques as using an eye dropper to apply water "when no one is around."

As for Father Bruse and the Lake Ridge statue weepings, Nickell leans heavily for his findings upon a venomous article which appeared April 24, 1992, in *The Washington City Paper*, a free weekly rag available to persons in Washington, DC. Written by Weston Kosovo, the article rambles around previous frauds, spends almost as much time criticizing *The Washington Post* for being too accepting of the evidence, and hints that all would be exposed if only a skeptic could examine the hollow, fiberglass Our Lady of Smiles statue. He seems oblivious to the fact that the weeping of other statues and images, about which he basically snorts derisively, eliminates the hollow interior of Our Lady of Smiles as a possible explanation for the phenomenon. His agenda is so obvious that the only reason to keep reading is to see whom he will pillory next. If you find this kind of yellow journalism convincing, you probably wasted your money if you paid for this book.

I have read a lot of critical articles about Fr. Bruse and the SEAS weepings. I have yet to find one which even begins to consider the actual evidence. These diatribes do nothing for discovering the truth. They merely disclose the negative biases of their authors and expose some astonishingly poor evidentiary analysis.

Further, Joe Nickell and his ilk are absolutely clueless about the ways of God. One would do as well to explain modern political science to aborigines as to get Nickell, Gardner, Sagan (before he died), Kosovo and others like them to understand the relationship of God with humanity. And quoting nervous, skeptical clerics doesn't help either. If you want a rational explanation that makes perfect sense, see Fr. Bruse's comments in the Epilogue to this book.[4]

Q: Some critics have suggested that making statues weep is trivial and, therefore, not something to which the Creator of the universe would stoop. They complain that the God who destroyed Sodom and Gomorrah, parted the Red Sea, inflicted plagues upon Egypt, and the like, would show Himself only in far more awesome demonstrations. How do you respond to this?

A: It strikes me as remarkably arrogant for a person, especially one who is almost always agnostic, if not outright atheistic, to presume to speak for God. In any event, such a comment demonstrates a woeful ignorance about the God worshipped in the Judeo-Christian faith.

The Book of Kings in the Old Testament, specifically 1 Kings 19, includes a direct refutation of this so-called triviality argument. Elijah the prophet, hiding in a cave from the Israelites, is told by God to wait for Him outside on the mountain, where the "Lord will be passing by."

> "A strong and heavy wind was rending the mountains and crushing
> rocks before the Lord—but the Lord was not in the wind. After the
> wind there was an earthquake—but the Lord was not in the

---

[4]Nickell can't get even his own facts straight. In note 33 to his chapter on "Magical Icons," he lists the date of his certified letter to Fr. Bruse, asking to examine the Our Lady of Smiles statue, as being May 29, 1991, six months before the weeping began.

earthquake. After the earthquake there was fire—but the Lord was not in the fire. After the fire there was a tiny whispering sound. When he heard this, Elijah hid his face in his cloak and went and stood at the entrance of the cave."[5]

We could hardly ask for more explicit authority that God comes to us in very quiet, insignificant ways rather than dramatic, earth-shaking events.

In the New Testament, God Himself, in the person of Jesus Christ, Second Person of the Holy Trinity, comes to earth not as king and conqueror, nor even high priest, but as a lowly carpenter. His followers are told to take the Ten Commandments one step further by living the eight beatitudes, guidelines which emphasize meekness, suffering, mercy and simplicity.[6] Tears are far more compatible with the God portrayed in these passages than the fire-and-brimstone deity advanced by men who seem to have confused the true God with Thor, the old Scandinavian god who inspired the Vikings to terrorize most of Europe.

Besides, what is trivial about tears? Most people respond to tears with sympathy or offers of assistance. Tears are passionate expressions of deep emotions, either for sorrow or happiness. They indicate quite reliably, usually, that something is seriously amiss. Why is this not the perfect way for God to communicate His distress through images of the Blessed Virgin Mary? What would these critics have her do? Throw things? Threaten? Yell?

Many people have been deeply moved by the sight of the statues shedding tears, or merely viewing the photos, or just hearing about it from reliable witnesses. The spiritual effects among those open to belief have been profound and have, indeed, demonstrated to these persons that God is real and present in our lives. This is hardly trivial.

As I said before, it would be easier to explain modern political science to aborigines than to get people who complain that weeping statues are trivial to begin to comprehend the nature of God.

Q: Isn't it true that the Catholic Church is often leery of this kind of phenomena and generally shys away from any association with it? Wouldn't it be better, then, for the faithful to also not pay any attention to such things?

---

[5]1 Kings 19:11-13

[6]Mt 5:3-12

A: In the case of Fr. Bruse and the physical phenomena which surrounded him, the Ordinary of the Diocese of Arlington, Bishop John R. Keating, did choose not to investigate. However, as I explained in the preface to this book, that decision seems clearly to have been wrongly based upon a notion that an apparition was required before an investigation would be warranted. As we can see from the famous weeping incident in Syracuse, Italy, in 1953, where Archbishop Baranzini appointed an investigative committee within days of learning about the weeping from a single image of the Blessed Virgin Mary, other episcopates have concluded differently about the value and timing of investigation. Today, in Syracuse, there is a huge, 11,000-capacity church to commemorate this four-day weeping event. Pope John Paul II himself officiated at the dedication of the Shrine of Our Lady of Tears (Fig. 13). So the Catholic Church is not organizationally opposed to association with miraculous physical phenomena.

The Church, however, should be prudent. Its assignment by Christ is to be His Mystical Body in the world and to convey the teachings of Jesus, as given to us by His apostles, interpreting them for the benefit of the faithful throughout history. It is important that private revelations, no matter how presented, not be confused with this mission of the Church. Nonetheless, if God chooses to reinforce the message of the Gospels from time to time, surely we all have an obligation to listen, to assess, and to heed. The surest test of any private revelation is whether it is consistent with the teachings of the Church. If it is, then the only task remaining is to verify that, in fact, it comes from God and is not the product of natural causes or fraud or other non-miraculous source. If it meets this test, too, then it should be declared by the Church, "worthy of belief by the faithful." This appellation has been granted many times in the past, including Syracuse, Lourdes, La Salette, Fatima, Beauraing and Banneux. It should be granted in the case of the weepings, etc., at Lake Ridge and elsewhere in connection with Fr. Bruse. To borrow a line used in political circles, in determining whether the phenomena here were miraculous: "If it looks like a duck, walks like a duck, and quacks like a duck, it is safe to say that it is a duck." Images of the Blessed Virgin Mary and Jesus which shed tears and bleed without natural explanation can safely be considered miraculous signs from a concerned God.

Q: But nearly everyone who tasted the tear water reported it to be without taste. In other words, it was not the composition of human tears, as was the case at Syracuse. Doesn't this mean that we cannot call the water "tears" and that it was not a miraculous phenomenon intended to represent actual crying by the Blessed Virgin Mary?

A: Inanimate, anhydrous objects do not produce water, whether from the eyes or elsewhere. When they do, it is worthy of investigation to find out why. Water which comes from the eyes of these figures represents tears. Toy makers have made dolls for decades which, through various mechanical means, emit "tears" for the benefit of little girls playing make believe. No one challenges the effectiveness of these toys on the basis of whether the tear water has the same composition as real tears. Even the children recognize that the doll's tear water is symbolic of a real person's tears.

The Madonna statues, crucifixes, and other religious icons are symbols of real personages. When these images emit water from the eyes, they represent the tears of the real beings who are not physically present. That is the message for us. Jesus and Mary are weeping. That message came through loud and clear in the weepings surrounding Father Bruse. It would not have been any different if the tear water had the composition of human tears.

Father Bruse reported that on a few occasions the tear water did taste salty to him. Be that as it may, the addition of human tear composition to the phenomena merely adds another element of inexplicability. There is already an overwhelming case for the miraculous here. It is not necessary that one more element be added to make the case convincing.

Q: In scientific experiments, people under hypnosis have produced blisters and burn effects in their bodies simply from the power of suggestion. Historically, there have been cases of stigmata wounds which appear to have been caused by the deeply disturbed personalities of some of the people exhibiting them. Couldn't this apply to Father Bruse as well?

A: The stigmata wounds borne by Fr. Bruse are more subjective than the weeping statues, but they were visible for awhile (Fig. 2) and they did bleed. Doctors who examined him were perplexed as to how this could happen since the wounds were not open ones like those which afflicted Padre Pio and which bled much more constantly. Some people reported the scent of roses in Fr. Bruse's vicinity when his wounds were bleeding. When the bleeding stopped, the wounds did not scab over. Before the wounds appeared in his own body, he was completely unfamiliar with the phenomenon. A psychiatrist who examined him found him to be completely normal in every respect with no indications of any personality traits which might produce such a profound reaction in his body.

Anyone who has known Father Bruse at all quickly realizes that he does not fit the mold of the mystical, hysterical or deeply obsessive personality of many past stigmatics. On the contrary, he has said that before his encounters with the supernatural, his own faith was weakening. Now he comes across as open, sincere and possessing of an uncomplicated kind of old-fashioned faith of the type more common in the 1950s when religious statues, holy water fonts, Catholic schools and stay-at-home moms were the stuff of everyday lives.

In the final analysis, however, the stigmata wounds of Fr. Bruse were authenticated by God Himself. Such an extraordinary display of objective, inexplicable phenomena of hundreds of religious statues, crucifixes and images weeping, color changes in many of these, rose fragrance where there were no flowers and no other possible source for such a scent, signs in the sun, and statue animation indicates that the stigmata came from the same supernatural source which directed these other manifestations.

Q: In September 1995, there were world-wide reports of the miraculous consumption of milk by the Hindu god, Ganesha, god of wisdom and learning. Reportedly, some other Hindu idols were involved as well. This phenomenon lasted about four days and was reported throughout the world, viewed by Hindu believers, the media, and skeptics alike. Doesn't this undercut the religious significance of the weeping statues and other phenomena which surrounded Father Bruse?

A: To begin with, I do not know how solid the evidence of this milk-drinking phenomenon actually was. There may be possible natural explanations for it. But let's assume it was genuinely miraculous (meaning involving a suspension of the normal laws of science). On its most basic level, it is a spiritual communication to Hindus, estimated to be as many as one billion people worldwide, reminding them that the supernatural world is real. For them, as the weeping Madonna statues are for Christians, the miraculous phenomena are reminders that we are more than material beings with physical desires and needs. We have immortal souls. That spiritual dimension must be given greater importance than is generally the case in the modern world, no matter what one's religion. In fact, sympathetic Hindu media noted that the popular response to the apparent milk-drinking miracle was a revival of religious belief. To the extent that these beliefs encourage Hindus to live their lives in ways that God would approve, this is a good thing.

Still, we know there is one Truth and that is the truth revealed by Jesus Christ, the Son of God and Second Person of the Holy Trinity, who, together, are One God. Christians are monotheistic, as are Jews and Muslims. Hinduism is a complex, polytheistic religion with multiple gods and idols, although it, too, has a kind of Trinity concept.

The fact that miracles occur in other religions is a reminder of two important facts: one, that God loves all of His human creation and calls all to worship Him in accordance with His principles of love and service. Two, our faith must rest upon the truths revealed by God. We are followers of Jesus Christ because He proclaimed himself to be the Son of God and then rose from the dead to prove it. His teachings and sacraments, especially the Eucharist, sustain us in our daily lives and explain our place in the universe. Weeping statues and similar phenomena remind us of this spiritual relationship, but our faith rests upon an entirely different basis. If God permits miraculous phenomena to occur in other faiths, it is not to attest to the truths of those faiths but to ensure that our own faith continues to be based upon the revelation of Jesus Christ, and the teachings of the Catholic Church down through the centuries. In other words, God is not interested in worshippers who proclaim, "I am a Catholic follower of Jesus Christ because I saw a statue weep tears." God demands our faith. The truest miracle is that He rewards that faith with personal signs of His presence and love if we but persist in our worship and live according to His commandments and guidance.

Even to Christians, however, there may be significance in the Hindu milk-drinking phenomenon. To Hindus, such a miracle is a sign that a "Great Soul" has been born. This Great Soul might be anti-Christian in some significant way. In that case, we should recall Mt 24:24 where we are warned that "false messiahs and false prophets will appear, performing signs and wonders so great as to mislead even the chosen if that were possible." Of course, the Great Soul, if that is what is portended by the milk-drinking phenomenon and still assuming that there is a supernatural cause for it, may be someone like Mahatma Gandhi, one who will bring peace, harmony and spiritual enlightenment to India.

Another possibility of the significance of this phenomenon rests in the fact that milk is food and a sign of fertility. God promised to our Jewish ancestors a "land flowing with milk and honey." These little Hindu idols consuming great quantities of milk may be a sign that fertility will be taken away, a warning of a great famine. Could there be any connection between this sign and the nuclear weapon tests performed by India this year? Certainly radioactivity is the opposite of fertility and has the potential to destroy life on a wide scale.

We do well to remember the lessons from the Book of Job. There Satan scoffed at God's pride in the uprightness of Job and challenged Him to let him make life a lot tougher for Job. Then "surely he will blaspheme you to your face," claimed Satan. (Jb 1:11). Job ultimately lost his family, all his wealth, and his health. But he did not denounce God. He kept his faith. Although he challenged the fairness of God, he was told, in essence, that some things are simply beyond his understanding and belong to the prerogatives of God, Creator of the universe.

So we, too, must accept with gratitude the signs which God gives us and use them to bolster our faith and renew the fervor and conviction with which we worship God. It is easy to imagine Satan saying to God that our faith which has been stimulated by witnessing weeping statues and similar miracles will not endure if God permits similar signs in other religions... and God responding, well, let's find out. The basis of our faith has not changed in 2,000 years. We should merely understand it better. And it has nothing to do with whether statues weep or not.

WHAT DOES IT ALL MEAN?

"A mother weeps when she sees her children threatened by evil, be it spiritual or physical." Pope John Paul II

If you see someone crying, what is your first reaction? Isn't it to ask, "What's wrong?" We automatically know that something is amiss—perhaps an injury to body or emotions, or perhaps a loss of some other grievous kind. At least ninety-five percent of us will feel a certain alarm when we see a person crying because we will assume that something bad has happened and it might be very serious.

It baffles me, then, that some people can seriously argue that without an apparition to explain things, weeping statues of the Blessed Virgin Mary are meaningless. Surely their meaning is overwhelmingly obvious. Heaven is upset about something, or perhaps many things. If we cannot figure out what those things are, then we are in even greater trouble than we might imagine for it would mean that we have absolutely lost our moral and spiritual compass.

Miraculous signs such as statues weeping, whether tears or oil, and occasionally bleeding, are at the very least generous gifts to bolster our weak faith. They are evidence of the existence and presence of a personal God who is trying to get our attention. If you draw no other conclusion than this, you have already gained most of the value of such signs—provided you act on the information and come back to church, to the Sacraments, and to faithful obedience to the commandments of God. Then, like the 3,000 converts on Pentecost Sunday, we can joyfully acknowledge that the greatest miracle is not the signs and wonders, but the conversion in the heart which transforms and saves the soul.

Nonetheless, tears are a specific form of communication. They tell of distress and sorrow. It is possible to cry for happiness, but the modern world is clearly not something which any resident of God's kingdom would be happy about. Let's consider some specifics for this indictment.

First, however, we should consider what it is that would upset the Blessed Virgin Mary and her Son, Jesus Christ, Son of God, who redeemed mankind at a terrible price in His own blood and pain. Clearly they love us with a depth of love that most of us here on earth can barely comprehend, much less imitate. So they will not wish to see us suffer unnecessarily. But suffering can be redemptive and Christ told us specifically that we must each take up our cross and follow Him if we wish to be His disciples. Still, this does not mean that God wishes us to suffer. Clearly, He desires that we do all in our power to ameliorate the sufferings of others. But, living as we do in a "vale of tears," there is plenty of opportunity to join our own sufferings with those of Christ as a sin offering for the benefit of all. This is a precious and generous gift in the sight of the Lord. It unites us with His Son. Such offerings form our heart in charity and draw us closer to God, who is Love itself. So the beauty of the spiritual equation is that all parts of our lives, even the suffering, can work together for the benefit of all. Thus, we can confidently say that the Blessed Virgin Mary is not weeping because there is too much voluntarily accepted suffering on earth. On the contrary, Mary has said explicitly:

> "*I have prevented the coming of calamities by offering Him the sufferings of the Son on the Cross, His Precious Blood, and beloved souls who console Him and form a cohort of victim souls. Prayer, penance and courageous sacrifices can soften the Father's anger.*"[1]

It also seems unlikely that Heaven is crying over natural disasters, such as hurricanes and earthquakes. Although these can wreak terrible destruction sometimes, we call them "acts of God" precisely because they are strictly within the control of nature as created by God. Violence by the planet with its loss of life and property is an essential part of the existence which we have following the Fall of Man. The Good News of Jesus Christ addressed the fact that death here is but a passage to a far more beautiful eternal existence elsewhere—provided we have lived lives compatible with the God of Love.

But wars, crime, abortion, child abuse, terrorism and oppression are not part of God's plan in any way. In this century, mankind has slaughtered itself to the tune of well over one billion![2] The ready availability of nuclear weapons and widespread acceptance of abortion threaten to increase this number geometrically.

---

[1] Haffert, John M., *The Meaning of Akita*, Asbury, NJ: 101 Foundation, 1993, p. 7.

[2] Estimates of deaths include approximately 9 million in WWI, 55 million in WWII, 20-30 million in the Russian pogroms of the 1930's, 50-60 million Chinese in the civil war won by the Communist Mao, millions in Cambodia in the 1970's, millions in China and Spain before WWII started, millions cumulatively in all the smaller wars around the globe, including Korea, Vietnam, Afghanistan, Rwanda, Iraq/Iran, the Persian Gulf War and insurrections in Central and South America, Northern Ireland and Angola. The balance of the estimate is from the undeclared, world-wide war on preborn babies, which takes the lives of an estimated 50-60 million per year from surgical abortion alone. The one billion number does not include the hundreds of millions of lives terminated by contraceptive abortifacients, pills which operate to prevent the uterus from being able to host a fertilized egg.

Surely that is reason for the Blessed Mother to weep and to weep tears of blood. Her messages at Akita, Japan, were quite specific in warning of incomprehensible destruction from fire which would fall from the sky:

> *"As I told you, if men do not repent and better themselves, the Heavenly Father will inflict a terrible punishment on all humanity. It will definitely be a punishment greater than the deluge, such as one will never have seen before. Fire will fall from the sky and will wipe out a great part of humanity... the good as well as the bad, sparing neither priests nor faithful."*[3]

This translation from the Japanese involves God in a severely hostile action more directly than the quote on pp. 88-89 in the chapter, "Statue Weepings Around the World," which is taken from Jan Connell's book, *Meetings with Mary*. To some, it may portray God in a harsh light and seem somewhat inconsistent with the notion of God as Love, as the father of the prodigal son, and Christ's admonition to Saint Peter to forgive "seventy times seven." (Mt 18:21-22). Yet, if considered from the perspective of our eternal souls, one can understand that there comes a point when the loss of so many souls due to the wholesale disregard of the commandments of God is worse than simply destroying the lot and letting humanity begin again. This was the situation at the Deluge. It is an action necessary to protect the souls of children being born into a world which will corrupt them, rather than help them save their souls. It is analogous to the horrible dilemma a parent might have in a situation where one child had taken all of his siblings hostage and was about to kill them. If the parent had the opportunity to intervene, it might be necessary to destroy the one child in order to save the others. Sinful man, of course, is much less able to make this judgment than the infinite and perfect God. In this light, the intervention of the Blessed Mother and the assistance she has received from people who fast and otherwise offer some sacrifice to atone for sins has maintained a level of grace in the world which has kept it from reaching this critical, hopeless stage. Given what we know of history, especially in this century, we will do well to not worry about the actions of our loving God and focus, instead, upon the enormous dangers we have created for ourselves. One way to view the tidal wave of sin and excess which has swept the

---

[3] *The Meaning of Akita*, p. 7; see also, Fukushima, Francis Mutsuo, *Akita: Mother of God as CoRedemptrix, Modern Miracles of Holy Eucharist,* Santa Barbara, CA:Queenship Publishing Co., 1994, pp. 14-15; and *Signs and Wonders for Our Times,*v. 10, No. 2, Summer 1998, p. 12.

world is that it brings the evil in mankind to a critical mass which can then explode in a new fury of hatred and destruction. It is God's love which has kept this explosion from happening. But the Blessed Virgin Mary has warned us explicitly at Akita that it cannot be held off indefinitely unless we reform our lives.[4]

There is something, however, much worse than war, even nuclear war. That is the loss of souls to eternal separation from God. In fact, it seems safe to conclude that the tears of the Blessed Virgin Mary, if shed for the possibility that terrible wars or natural calamities may be about to ensue, are more for the loss of souls which would result than the loss of lives. A world steeped in sin to the point that new and more destructive conflicts may be about to erupt is a world in which large numbers of souls are in serious jeopardy of being lost forever. At Fatima, the Blessed Mother expressed her concern for the fate of sinners who had no one to pray and sacrifice for them, so that many were being lost to hell.[5] At Akita, in her last message to Sr. Agnes on October 13, 1973, the Blessed Virgin Mary specifically said to her:

> *"The thought of the loss of so many souls is the cause of my sadness. If sins increase in number and gravity, there will be no longer pardon for them."*[6]

Well, what are these terrible sins, some might ask. After all, is the world really so terrible a place? Aren't we all pretty much the way mankind has always been?

The basic raw material, human beings descended from Adam and Eve, is, indeed, pretty much the way it has always been. However, we have the advantage in the past 2,000 years of being post-Jesus Christ, which means we do not have to hang around in "Hades" waiting for the Gates of Heaven to swing open through the redemptive sacrifice of the Son of God. We also have the benefit of Christ's teachings about how to live our lives so that we will qualify to pass through those

---

[4]The translation offered by Jan Connell in *Meetings with Mary* may be more true to the spirit of the Blessed Mother's words. Either way, the message for us is the same: we must pray constantly, fast regularly or offer up some other sacrifice to help to atone for the sins of the world, and work tirelessly to live the lives of love and service to which Jesus called us.

[5]August 13, 1917 apparition.

[6]*The Meaning of Akita,* p. 8.

Gates. Here is a two-edged sword, however. Knowing the way we are expected to live makes our transgressions that much worse. In other words, we have less of an excuse than pre-Christians had. We have the New Testament to instruct us. We also have graces and divine assistance available to us through the Sacraments, especially the Eucharist, that non-Christians, before and after Christ, can only envy. How much worse, then, for Catholics, and other Christians, too, when we spurn these advantages and neglect the commandments of God.

Certainly a major commandment of God is the Fifth Commandment: "*Thou shalt not kill.*" The prohibition is not absolute. Defense of self and others is permitted. But there is no exception for killing the defenseless. There is no class more defenseless than preborn children. And calling them "fetuses" and "zygotes" and other scientific jargon does not change the reality that they are human beings. The sin of abortion is like a great black cloud of stinking smoke rising from the earth to obscure the loving gaze of Heaven. Not since pagan times has this sin been so widespread and common.

According to her message at Akita, the Blessed Virgin Mary weeps primarily for the loss of souls. Nothing that happens on this earth—absolutely nothing—even begins to compare to the tragedy of losing your soul for all eternity. Yet we live in a time when only 10% of German Catholics attend Sunday Mass regularly, and percentages in other parts of Europe are comparable. In the Czech Republic, 40% of the population claims to be atheistic! In Latin America, church attendance, especially by men, is equally abysmal. The Church has always taught that the willful failure to worship God by faithful Sunday Mass attendance is a mortal sin. So where is it likely that the souls of these people are going if they do not repent before they die? Where will the souls of these millions of people go if their lives are suddenly snuffed out in some great nuclear or natural cataclysm? And we wonder why the Blessed Virgin Mary weeps for us.

As far as sexual conduct is concerned, we live in a full-blown neo-pagan society where sexual intercourse is viewed by many, especially in the entertainment industry, as a natural concomitant to dating. In the United States, nearly 40% of ninth graders have had sexual intercourse at least once. The percentages rise to 46%, 55% and 68%, respectively, for the tenth, eleventh and twelfth grades of high school. Sexual activity is occurring at younger and younger ages. No wonder sexual diseases are rampant. Popular television series like "Friends," "Seinfeld," "Frasier," "ER," and "Ally McBeal" portray sexual activity completely free of any spiritual dimension. These shows, of course, are tame compared to some of the overtly sexual programs, of which there are many.

The Census Bureau reported in July 1998 that unwed heterosexual pairs living together now make up more than four million American households, an eightfold increase since 1970. Analyzing the statistics, *The Washington Post* reported:

> "The figures reflect a broad social change: a practice that was rare and widely rejected as immoral not long ago has now become common. Other research shows that half of women in their early thirties have lived with a man outside of marriage."[7]

But sex outside marriage has been severely condemned in numerous places in the New Testament. At your leisure, check out the passages at Mt 15:19-20, 7:21-22; Acts 21:25; 1 Cor 6:9, 18; Gal 5:19; Eph 5:3, 5-6; 1 Thes 4:3-5; Heb 13:4; Rev 21:8; Rev 22:14-15.

We also have the explicit comment of the Blessed Virgin Mary herself. Jacinta, one of the three children to see the apparitions at Fatima, said, apparently in response to an inquiry which she made to the Mother of God, that the kind of sin which offends God most are sins of the flesh.[8] And we wonder why the Blessed Virgin Mary weeps for us.

Before we leave the phenomena of the statue signs, and turn to the stigmata of Father Bruse, let us consider some of the things that we can be sure were *not* signified by those miraculous activities:

•   They were not provided for our amusement. These are very serious signs portending great dangers (not necessarily physical) with the highest stakes: our immortal souls.

•   They were not intended to stimulate sales of religious goods or even necessarily the acquisition of religious icons, although that is a salutary response to these signs.

•   They were not indications that we should worship statues of the Blessed Virgin Mary as if she were really present inside them. These little statues only represent her; our minds and our prayers must distinguish between symbol and the reality which is in Heaven, albeit readily accessible to us through prayer.

•   They were not intended to be substitutes for the principles of our faith. God does not wish us to attend church because He made statues cry. Faith is still the garment of our salvation. Statues, no matter what they do, do not

---

[7] July 27, 1998, Section A.

[8] *Fatima in Lucia's Own Words,* p. 107.

explain why we follow Jesus Christ. If the tears of Mary have called you back to the Church, then come back fully. Participate in the Mass regularly and faithfully; make frequent use of the Sacrament of Reconciliation; read Scripture; learn the elements of your faith; pray, pray and pray, especially the daily rosary. Then her vicarious tears will have truly accomplished their purpose.

• They were not intended to lead us into bomb shelters, mountains or caves to escape possible disasters. Even if such things lie in our future, we must place our trust in the loving custody of Christ and His Blessed Mother and try now to live our lives as they would have us live them and to share Christ's message with others so that they, too, may discover the joy and salvation which Jesus offers to all mankind. It is our souls which are important, not our bodies. If the Blessed Virgin Mary is warning us of physical dangers, it is because sudden death may catch us spiritually unprepared. That is the real tragedy. At Akita, Mary said, *"Those who place their confidence in me will be saved."*[9] There is our shelter.

Let us remember, too, some of the other signs: statues and rosaries changing colors, statues becoming animated, heavenly rose fragrance, and the beautiful sun signs. These are reminders of the beauty, joy and reality of heaven—which God is anxious to share with His children: you, me and all the other members of the human race. They also reassure us that we are made in the image and likeness of God, that we are more lost and confused than evil, that in the world there is still love and joyous celebration, there is still goodness and courage, there is still dignity and respect, there is still hope.

Father Bruse's stigmata wounds mark him as exceptionally worthy of our attention. They are signs of God's special interest in him. Where God will lead him or what He will have him do in the future, none of us can know and we should not waste time speculating about it. The important lesson for us is to evaluate what about Fr. Bruse may be part of the message of God to us.

Personally, I believe that the character and personality of Father Bruse are part of the message itself. God, especially through the apparitions of the Blessed Mother, often chooses the gentle and unassuming as the instruments for divine revelations. The major apparitions at Lourdes, Fatima and Medjugorje have been to children. The humble and powerless magnify God's strength. Not to the clever and the wise does God reveal himself (Mt 11:25). Perhaps mankind's greatest sin, and Lord knows there is a great deal of competition for this award, is human

---

[9]*The Meaning of Akita*, p. 9.

pride—the arrogant, overconfident sense that we are masters of our own destiny and can conquer all frontiers with our technological wizardry. What better instrument for a "wake-up call" then, than a simple, unpretentious priest who claims no profound theological insights, loves nature and is almost completely guileless?[10] He is a powerful reminder that we who pride ourselves in our intellectual capabilities, our clever way with words, our sophisticated *savoir faire* are only fooling ourselves. God calls us to simplicity. He calls us to listen and to love. He calls us to serve. He calls us to share our gifts generously and for the good of all, as He so immeasurably blesses each one of our lives, no matter how grim, by promising us eternal joy at the end of it. He calls us to value our priests for their God-granted ability to bring Christ to us in the Holy Eucharist. For these purposes, Father Bruse is the perfect instrument. His openness and, indeed, his vulnerability draw our hearts to a God who asks us to think of Him as something like "Daddy" (the Aramaic "Abba").

Finally, we have seen (see story of Audrey Santo in "Statue Weepings Around the World") that tears of oil may well signify healing. They remind us that the Holy Mother of God will be our consolation and help in abandoning our sinful ways and living the life to which we are called by our Lord Jesus Christ. Since the only statues at Lake Ridge which wept oil were the personal ones of Fr. Bruse, it seems likely that God's message in this phenomenon is that Fr. Bruse will be an instrument in bringing the Blessed Virgin Mary's healing to souls.

---

[10]This is not to suggest that Father Bruse is an ineffective homilist. On the contrary, there is an extraordinary power which comes through him: the power of truth and directness but contained in a gentleness which speaks eloquently of the love which God has for us. One gets the strong impression that he speaks of things which he has seen. His convictions of the reality of Christ and reassurances to us of His love and concern dispel fear like fog blown before a breeze.

EPILOGUE

I began this journal at a time when not many people were aware of the weeping statues, stigmata of Fr. Bruse and other phenomena which had begun only two months earlier. At that time, no one was making a formal effort to record the events for accuracy and posterity. It seemed to me that it was vitally important that this be done so that others who were not so fortunate as to be eyewitnesses to the events would at least have a comprehensive summary of what transpired here. Later, the reaction of my high school religious education students and friends with whom I shared these stories made me realize that all of us have an obligation to share this news with anyone who may be interested and seeking affirmation of their faith in God. Physical miracles are thrilling to behold, but they have little value, truly, unless they lead souls to conversion and to God. The most wonderful thing about a miracle is that this spiritual benefit can be shared by all who learn of it, not merely the direct beneficiary.

Amy Shaffer said it best: "*It is not our miracle. It is a miracle which needs to be shared.*"

The material presented in these pages involves so many events and so many people in so many diverse locations as to be overwhelmingly convincing. Adding even more stories and case histories is fascinating and worthwhile, but somewhat redundant also. Unless Our Lady manifests herself here in an entirely new way, it falls to us now to ponder the significance of what has happened here. There is no better way to do this than to consider Fr. Bruse's own words on the subject. These excerpts are from a talk he gave to the SEAS high school religious education teachers on February 7, 1993:

> "My faith was fluctuating. Priests get that way. Sometimes Mass can become a normal routine and this just smashed all of that. To see it move into a very deep thing, where people are converting, who have been away from church 15, 20, 30 years... I do believe in the reality of Christ! It's changed my whole life around, in many ways, in many beautiful ways.

> "I'm trying to get the people now to look beyond the signs, to see where their faith is now, and see where they're going to go with this. This parish has been touched in a very special way. We've been blessed to have seen something like this, to have experienced it. You don't have to doubt Christ anymore. You don't have to doubt where we're going after we die. God is real!

> "Jesus is saying to us, 'Let them know that I am real. Let them know that I am waiting for them to come to me.'

"A lot of people that I've talked to no longer come to Mass and sit there and think of other things. They come there and they get something from the Mass because they're open to it. These physical phenomena have helped that way, they definitely have. It's opened people's hearts. It's letting people know what's happening, especially in the Sacrifice of the Mass.

"Know that Christ is real. You don't have to doubt anymore. Christ is real! You don't have to doubt your prayers. You don't have to doubt the Holy Sacrifice of the Mass. Christ is there. He's very much real. You don't have to doubt the Kingdom of God—heaven. It's all confirmed by what's happened. Take that faith in Jesus and keep it alive in your hearts.

"And Mary is there with you, too. Mary is the model for the Church. She can help us. She can intercede. She's done that for us here in this church many times.

"Keep an open heart. Share your love with Christ. He's listening to you. He's definitely listening to you!

"We can be changed for the rest of our lives if we just turn to Christ and say we believe you and we love you."

PRAYER OF POPE JOHN PAUL II
TO MADONNA OF THE TEARS

O Lady of Tears,
look with motherly goodness
on the sorrow of the world!
Dry the tears of the suffering,
of the forgotten, of the desperate
and of the victims of every violence.
Make everyone weep tears of repentance
and of new life,
which will open their hearts
to the regenerating gift
of God's love.
Make them weep tears of joy
for having seen
the profound tenderness
of your heart.
Amen.

Appendix A

<u>CHANCERY STATEMENT ISSUED TO FR. DANIEL HAMILTON, PASTOR OF ST. ELIZABETH ANN SETON PARISH, LAKE RIDGE.</u>

The staff of St. Elizabeth Ann Seton Parish, Lake Ridge, has informed the Diocesan Chancery regarding various reported physical phenomena associated with a variety of statues and crucifixes in the parish.

It should be pointed out that the Church does not pass judgment on purely physical phenomena, but only on a purported meaning, message or significance that may be associated with the events.

In this particular case there is no determined message attached to the reported physical phenomena, and thus there is no ecclesial declaration to be made at this time.

As always in similar cases, the Church recommends great caution in forming judgments, and advises against any speculation on the causes or possible significance of the reported events.

RECEIVED MARCH 5, 1992

Appendix B

PASTORAL LETTER FROM FATHER PAUL BURNS

[This is a copy of the pastoral letter which Father Paul Burns, pastor of Our Lady of Angels parish in Woodbridge, Virginia, wrote to his parish on March 25, 1992. It appeared in the church bulletin the following Sunday, March 29.]

<u>NOTE FROM FR. PAUL:</u>   March 25, 1992

Last weekend at Mass I had a few comments about recent events here in connection with the statue of Our Lady in the Narthex. . .<u>final public comments</u>, because we need to get on with our usual Sacramental practices, increasing and bettering our participation in them. For those who attended other Masses, this is a summary.

The facts: on Tuesday, March 17, while Fr. Bruse, stationed at SEAS in Lake Ridge, was celebrating Mass in our church as part of a scheduled rotation of local priests for that Mass, the statue of Mary was noticed to have water flowing down from the face over the bodice and to the sides. . .water suggestive of tears. The flowing water was witnessed by many adults. Moisture on the statue was seen by about four hundred children also, as they hesitated at the statue while leaving Mass. When I returned from northern Virginia that day, about twenty minutes after the Mass was over, I also witnessed tears on the statue.

The events are not directly connected with our church. As you know, these things have been happening in connection with Fr. Bruse at SEAS. It <u>did</u> happen to <u>our</u> statue, however, involving us indirectly. We did not seek out any publicity about this, of course. A necessary letter was prudently sent home with the pupils of Aquinas School, to help separate fact from imaginative fiction. Some folks called the press, (no problem with that) and then the "media event" was on. We tried to be courteous and cooperative with the various reporters, and to help keep the facts straight. After about five or six interviews, I stopped talking to reporters because, despite all good intentions, the editing process often caused my words to be cast in meanings I did not intend. What is <u>left out</u> of interviews often is more important than what is put in!

The causes of these events are not known at present by anyone. Neither has any definite significance been attached to the phenomena. Are they God breaking through the crust of our usual human experience? Is the cause an as yet unexplained natural factor. . .a preternatural event? Is it of supernatural origin?

Who would be so bold as to deny that possibility altogether? Personally, I am certain, as are so many others, that the cause is not fraudulent in any way.

The church has historically been very cautious about such phenomena, and slow to pronounce anything about them. They are in the area of private revelation, which is not binding on anyone in terms of belief. You can be a total skeptic, a believer, or undecided about a purported private revelation, in perfectly good conscience. The only ones who would be bound by a private revelation are those to whom it is directly given. This would include even Lourdes, Fatima and others to which the Church has given approbation. The only revelation we are bound to is that of the Sacred Scriptures and the official teachings of our Church.

The church has never officially pronounced on the <u>causes</u> of these phenomena. Sometimes, if there is a definite message connected with them (there is none as yet with these events around Fr. Bruse), the Church will, after a long examination, officially comment on the meaning. In all cases when there has been a clear message connected with an apparition, it has been something we already know or believe, and is in the form of a reminder to "get it together!" Sometimes, the Church <u>repudiates</u> the possibility of anything genuinely religious concerning an event; sometimes, it lets the events pass without <u>any</u> <u>comment</u> at all.

There is always a concern that these happenings will be turned into circuses by people who want to make some kind of hay out of them, either spiritual or monetary. Often subjective interpretations multiply, and lead to hysterical reactions. Sometimes, people who seem to have a certain need to frighten other people, promote these events as "divine threats." Chain letters are an example of this. They are an especially damnable form of superstition because, while presuming to tell God how to run his world, they usually imply that the Creator is some kind of capricious tyrant, who will hit you over the head with a disaster if you do not follow the directions. We have enough people ridiculing religion these days without giving them more fodder for their cannons. If you receive a chain letter in <u>any</u> form, do not participate in this violation of the First Commandment. It is a virtuous act to trash such things and forget about their contents.

Then there is always that old accusation, that Catholics "worship" statues. While some Catholics have sometimes given the impression that we "pray to statues," the clear teaching of the Church is that the statue is a mere reminder of Our Lady or of a saint whom we respect as someone who lived, in their everyday life, in faithful imitation of Christ, and we ask them for help in that respect, i.e., to help us imitate the Master. Let's make sure that we keep this all in perspective, lest we be guilty of furthering such a ridiculous proposition.

Finally, I am glad that most of our people are viewing these events in a positive light. The children saw them as a blessing. I think we all should; and each one take whatever meaning there will be in it for us, as an actual grace in our lives. Above all, let us not be distracted from the core of our faith and practice. All Sacramentals (statues, blessings, etc.) exist to deepen our Sacramental life; that is where our main attention forever lies as a church. We should all keep up with our usual Lenten practices of prayer and self-discipline which will lead us to the high point of Easter, the personal, public renewal of our Baptismal Promises, and a new lease on our life with Christ.